BEING THE CHANGE

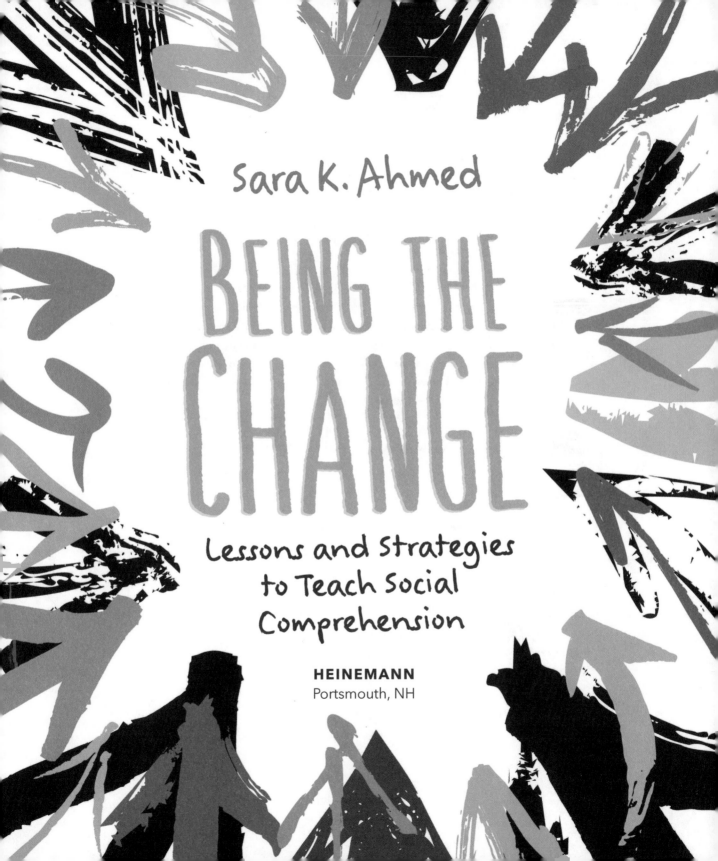

Sara K. Ahmed

BEING THE CHANGE

Lessons and Strategies to Teach Social Comprehension

HEINEMANN
Portsmouth, NH

Heinemann
361 Hanover Street
Portsmouth, NH 03801–3912
www.heinemann.com

Offices and agents throughout the world

Cataloging-in-Publication Data is on file at the Library of Congress.
ISBN: 978-0-325-09970-5

Editor: Tobey Antao
Production editor: Patty Adams
Typesetter: Gina Poirier Design
Cover and interior designs: Suzanne Heiser
Interior photographer: Silampa Danchuwong
Manufacturing: Steve Bernier

Printed in the United States of America on acid-free paper

22 21 20 19 18 VP 1 2 3 4 5

To Mom and Dad
for showing me how to do little things
with big heart.

Hearts must change. [They] won't change overnight. Social attitudes oftentimes take generations to change. But if our democracy is to work the way it should in this increasingly diverse nation, then each one of us need[s] to try to heed the advice of a great character in American fiction, Atticus Finch, who said "You never really understand a person until you consider things from his point of view, until you climb into his skin and walk around in it."

–President Barack Obama
(Farewell Speech, Chicago, 2016)
& Atticus Finch (*To Kill a Mockingbird*
by Harper Lee, 1960)

CONTENTS

Chapter 1: Exploring Our Identities 1

Chapter 2: Listening with Love 30

Chapter 3: Being Candid 41

Foreword

By Terrence J. Roberts, PhD.

In "The Prophet," Kahlil Gibran reminds us that it is when you give of yourself that you truly give. This gift from Sara K. Ahmed embodies the essence of that thought. You will be motivated to return to these pages often as you discover the quality of the offering she has chosen to share. Her willingness to speak to us from the center of her being is borne of a desire to educate, stimulate, challenge, and open new pathways to truth and understanding. You, the reader, are called upon to be "as transparent as possible and make your thinking visible."

Sara models this behavior as she encourages you to be the change for your students; your choice to be an active learner will pay unseen dividends. As you walk into the classroom, your commitment to learning will be evident to all and sundry. If your level of commitment includes a willingness to do whatever it takes to learn how to connect with others at the deepest possible strata, your students will witness the drama of life unfolding before them in ways heretofore deemed impossible by many, cherished by all.

The tools provided in this monograph might best be considered as catalysts. Use them not as instruments to elicit desired outcomes but to stimulate thinking about issues and matters of import. As you follow Sara's suggestion to "muddle through these with your peers before you engage your students," you will develop even more skill and expertise. The focus will be less on covering the material and more on exploring aspects of the revealed content that have the most relevance for you and your students.

And, as if this were not enough, you have access to a toolkit that can travel with you however far you roam away from the classroom. Yes, the lessons imparted herein are applicable in every possible sphere of life. On the assumption that self is the basic tool in your kit, the enhancements gifted to you by Sara can be utilized in the service of creating a more nuanced, dynamic self. And, by my definition, any such self is compelled to learn the lessons life has to teach. And guess what? A lot of those lessons are waiting at the intersection of you and each one of your students.

Sara knows these things; she has lived this life, and she has decided to make her thinking visible in these pages. By doing so she pledges allegiance to yet another basic tenet of human interaction: she cares enough to confront. She has confronted and continues to confront herself, and now she confronts us, her readers, and asks the hard questions we need to answer.

Accept this gift in the spirit it was given, life giving unto life, in recognition of the fact that without each other we are far less than we could be, but with each other, there is no limit to what we can be, what we can become.

A Letter to Readers

On any given day of the week, faithful congregants are flowing in and out of a quaint church in a small town outside of Chicago. The stairs split upon entry the way a tri-level house does. A few lead upstairs and many more guide you down to the first floor. You inhale that church smell when you first walk in—the scent of hymn books and Bibles mixed with the earthiness of the solid oak pews, long absorbing the oils of many worshipping hands. The sounds of the building vary with the time and the day.

From worshippers climbing the split stairs:
"Good morning, Father."
"Go in peace."

From worshippers descending to the lower level:
"Aslaam-walaikum (Peace be with you), brother, sister."

From the prayer rugs on a Friday afternoon, the Adzhan, the Muslim call
*   to prayer.*
From the church altar, the songs and sermon of Sunday.
From all believers, hands folded, eyes closed,
Collective calls for unity. Collective sounds of trust and hope, echo from
*   that humble intersection of our little town.*

Dear Reader,

In this book we will be spending time learning about our own identities and the identities of others to grow a better understanding of our place in this world. I'd like to begin that journey by sharing a story with you.

On a crisp September day in 1972, a young couple from Bombay, India, deplaned at Chicago's O'Hare International Airport with a few suitcases, a pair of architectural degrees, a young baby girl in tow—and visas to boot. A love marriage with a story to write.

Emigrating to a suburban neighborhood of Chicago in the 1970s was an adjustment for a Muslim family from India. Their new reality held beautiful churches on the corners instead of mosques or temples, and the ringing of majestic bells in place of the Adzhan, the melodic call to prayer. I imagine it was culture shock to say the least.

A compassionate extrovert, my father, Hamid, held his own at the neighborhood and work parties he was invited to. As a Muslim, he politely refused the alcoholic drinks he was offered. Instead he impressed them with the Foxtrot and Chubby Checker moves he had picked up back in university in India. Hamid brought his sense of community, a group of people coming together in the spirit of something bigger than themselves, to every new experience. Immigrants have a beautiful way of seeking out what feels safe in a place of uncertainty.

Hamid met the other Muslims in the neighboring communities of their new home, listening to their stories and wishes. All of them were in search of a place to plant their small communal roots of the bigger American Dream, the opportunity to improve your life no matter who you are. My father has a contagious personality and a childlike optimism that can move mountains. He started holding prayer services out of our home. Then, with the arrival of two more daughters and a growing group, they ended up renting a space at the local community center. Word spread and they outgrew that space as well. Along the way, Hamid befriended Father Green, a reverend at a church in town. Friendship became partnership, and Father Green opened the doors of the church and the first floor of the building to area Muslims to hold their Friday prayers. I remember it as a place where my cousins and I would listen dutifully in summer school and then run across the street to indulge in Slurpees and nachos from 7-Eleven.

That was thirty-five years ago.

Today, through the aftershocks of 9/11, through the unsubstantiated rhetoric and fear spread by our media, through the protection of local law enforcement so worshippers can pray in peace, through the advocacy of Father Green and the new love and support of Father Rasicci, you still hear the harmonized melody of the church bells and the Adzhan.

Collective calls for unity

Collective sounds of trust and hope

echo from that humble intersection of our little town.

My parents had their annual trip to India planned for earlier this year. My mother canceled her trip out of fear after hearing the stories from others who were unable to return to the United States as a result of the new ban. My father still went; after all, no United States citizen should be stopped from seeing his family, right? But the muddled ambiguity of the ban gave rise to a new form of hysteria around us. And even though the ban was repealed, we know that one of the last places this type of discriminatory policy leaves is in the minds and dispositions of the people who have been charged with enforcing it and in those who have been reached by the fear-mongering sensationalism of the media.

The days leading up to his flight home we all called my dad. We talked him through what to say if he was questioned. We reminded him repeatedly to call us when he landed, and when he got his bags, and again when he was through customs. We were strategizing with him as if he were doing something wrong for taking a trip and coming home.

The day of his arrival, we anxiously await his text that he is safely on the ground. But it doesn't come. My mom, my sisters, and I text back and forth anxiously. We confirm that the flight has landed. We try calling him, but we can't get through. Why hasn't he contacted us? Why can't we contact him?

We know our father. We know that the problem could be a simple luggage delay or a dead phone battery. But as the minutes turn to hours, our worries intensify. I pause to remind myself that this is an American citizen landing in America. I can't believe we are buying into the idea of criminalizing my own father for flying on an airplane and reentering the land he has called *home* for over forty-five years. This is what fear does.

Finally, my mom texts: she has heard from him. He is fine.

I called my dad later that evening to welcome him back. He shared stories about my cousins and newborn babies in the family.

Then he said, "You know, Sara, I didn't say anything to your mom or sisters, because they will get upset, but they took me into a special security customs area."

All of my terror from earlier in the day flooded back. I pulled the phone away from my face, trying to regain composure, before responding.

"I wondered about that, Dad. It took so long for you to call us. . . . Are you OK?"

"Yeah, I am fine; they just made me sit and then talked to me and asked me where I was coming from and why. I told them I saw my family and I've gone every year for forty-five years to see my brothers. Then I told the officer it was the best time to visit India if he ever wants to go. I told him the weather is beautiful, about 75 degrees and sunny. Not too hot yet."

I smile on the other end of the phone at my father's childlike spirit. This is so him. "What did he say?"

"Well, then the officer gave me back my passport and said, 'Well, maybe someday I will go. Welcome home, sir,' and smiled. He was a nice young man, actually, Sara."

Through some silent tears, I muster the courage to ask him a question I didn't really want the answer to.

"What was the area like where they took you, Dad?"

"Well, it was just like a plain hallway full of Muslims."

In 2014, the Pew Center surveyed more than three thousand Americans on their familiarity with other religious groups. Of the three thousand–some respondents, 87 percent said they know someone who is Catholic, 61 percent know someone of the Jewish faith, and 38 percent know someone of Muslim faith.

That means 62 percent of Americans don't know a Muslim. They have only the media to inform their opinions about Muslims. At a time when researchers and journalists agree that Western media overwhelmingly portray Muslims and Islam negatively, it's easy to understand why so many Americans feel some form of fear when they hear the word *Muslim* or *Islam* or a name they think "sounds Muslim." They gaze, then avert their eyes from the visible Muslim classifications we equate with a threat, a hijab or headscarf, a man with a longer beard.

That is a lot of people who could be fearful of my father. Fearful before even getting the chance to see his baseball cap collection or play tennis with him, or hear the story of when he met the Dalai Lama—no cameras or phones allowed, yet when he got home, we all got a great view of his blurred thumb, and the Dalai Lama's left eyebrow and ear.

A hallway full of Muslims. An image I cannot unsee. My father and many others dehumanized in his own country for forty minutes . . . in that hallway full of Muslims. That was the first time I felt my own family's "citizenship" being delegitimized and saw how policies can render a person's humanity invisible. This othering sends a message, "you are not one of us." For the most part, my family has flown under the radar of "othering" in America. Many families in our school communities have felt the effects of othering or discrimination and persecution—for generations, day after day.

Doing the work of social comprehension erodes the boundaries between "us" and "them."

My father's life strategy is the heart and soul of this book: "You have to talk with people. Smile and be nice with them." He models it on a daily basis. Simple and quite effective if you're lucky enough to know him. And often this strategy works. Being kind, to everyone.

The year 2018 marks my sixteenth year as a student of the educational systems in our world. I have spent my career teaching and learning in public urban and suburban, private independent, charter, and international classrooms. What I have learned is that we cannot progress as a society if we rely on television images, single stories, and sensationalized headlines over getting proximate to the personal experiences and individual truths of human beings who don't look like us.

In his book *Minds Made for Stories* (2014), Tom Newkirk says we simply cannot translate bare numbers into recognizable human reality; our eyes glaze over. Newkirk calls on the power of storytelling, the narrative, as a way to emotionally identify with people we might see as outsiders. Doing the work of social comprehension erodes the boundaries between "us" and "them."

So here I am with you today, beginning with my father's story in hopes you will invite the narratives of your students into the safety of your learning environments. Together, if we heed his advice and "talk with people," we can shift from statistics to stories in the spirit of a more inclusive world. Because if we are listening closely, if we are being compassionate observers of the world, the stories implore us to examine and question and reflect on our own identities—whether we know it or not.

I thank you for the tireless work you continue to build toward *collective sounds of trust and hope* in our world and for including this book as one tool in the canon of your life's work with our kids. Thank you for being the change.

In peace, love, and solidarity, and with immense gratitude.

With Gratitude...

I learned early on that behind every author's name on the cover of a book there is *a village*. In my case, a very large village.

My village begins with my editor, Tobey Antao. I have asked her multiple times if we could add her name to the cover because we have grown so close over the years; I sometimes can't decipher between her edits and my own. She is my writing's best friend; she knows it inside and out, questions it with love, gives it the confidence it needs to be purposeful and meaningful for its readers. Most of our collaboration phone calls had an 11-hour time difference, where one of us was finishing dinner, the other breakfast. I had her morning energy, while she had my nighttime lag and barely coherent thoughts to work with. The relationship with your editor is a special one and I am an extremely lucky author.

Thank you, Tobey. For everything.

TO THE TEAM AT HEINEMANN:

To *Sarah Fournier* for always making me laugh over zoo talk and ensuring that no detail of this book's journey was missed;

to *Lisa Fowler* for your unparalleled compassion, vision, and for my birds;

to *Patty Adams* for your patience and loving attention to the production work on *Upstanders* and this project and for always having a soccer story ready for me;

to *Elizabeth Silvis* who took my very first (and favorite) official photo of me, Smokey, and *Upstanders* and for helping to craft the concept of this title;

to *Brett Whitmarsh*, the Presidential Suite of social media genius and more than anything, the greatest, warmest sounding board for me;

to *Lauren Audet*, for your optimism and ideas. Scratch and sniff *Being the Change* stickers are in our future;

to *Eric Chalek*, for your intentionality in asking thoughtful questions that long stayed with me as I wrote this book;

to *Suzanne Heiser*, you had me at our first design in 2014. Your eye holds no bounds. I am in love with this cover;

to *Sarah Weaver*, copyediting is no small feat. Thank you for making sure my I's are dotted, my T's are crossed, and there is no fake news in this book;

to *Sherry Day* and *Michael Grover*, for being with me cross-country and across the world; there's a confidence and comfort through the lens only you two could bring. We have all the fun;

to my Heinemann PD heroes: *Mim Easton, Cheryl Savage, Samantha Brown, Michelle Flynn, Donna Robillard* and *Jaclyn Karabinas*; I am able to do what I do because of your attentive hearts. Thank you for always being there for the silly things and the serious things. And for literally managing my life when I need it the most;

to *Vicki Boyd*, general manager at Heinemann. This one is hard to do without a few tears. For every single chat you have carved out the time to have. For the way you have helped raise me in this industry and in this world. The Dalai Lama says "Compassion is the radicalism of our time." You, Boss, are a radical.

This Heinemann family. They hold their authors up. They are like no other.

To my NIST village: I am lucky enough to learn on the job every single day with all of you. You make being a very small fish in a rather large pond across the world an absolute joy. Thank you for opening my eyes to our big world; it's incredibly humbling. To Beth Dressler, you had me at, "I have an idea" the day we met. Thank you for always dreaming. To Brett Penny, thank you for taking a chance on me. This chapter of my life would not be possible without your foresight and ability to create for change. To the kids, the world is so fortunate to have you as global citizens.

To my Burley School village: Not a day goes by when I don't thank my lucky stars that I landed in line at a Chicago Public Schools job fair in front of Principal Barbara Kent. There is an unparalleled magic in neighborhood public schools. Every teaching move, every professional text I read, every time I question and reflect on my practice, every moment I put kids first is because every single one of you. (Especially you, Mr. Dennis Gallagher, may you rest in peace.) To the kids, I am watching you grown up and active on the front lines for civil liberties and human rights. Using your voices, the pen, the medias. Wow. I am so proud.

To my Bishop's village: I opened my eyes a little wider because of so many of you. And I held the mirror up much closer because of a few of you, and for that, I am forever indebted. Marcus, David, José, Carlos, Muhammad, Cory, Meg, Jen and Carol. Thank you for starting the conversation for me.

To my Facing History and Ourselves village (Chicago, Los Angeles, Boston, New York, and London). Because of you all, my lens and measure of history is the human story. You have brought Dr. Terrence Roberts, Bryan Stevenson, Eboo Patel, survivors, artists, and upstanders into my life. You were my first professional development experience where I left asking more questions rather than feeling like I needed all the answers. Thank you for helping me realize that is how we grow as individuals.

To my village of professional mentors: To Nancie Atwell, Stephanie Harvey, Anne Goudvis, Debbie Miller, Linda Hoyt, Lucy Calkins, Mary Ehrenworth, Donalyn Miller, Kristin Ziemke, Katie Muhtaris, Nancy Steineke, Ralph Fletcher, Tanny McGregor, and Steven Zemelman. You are some of the first people I read, heard, and learned from and continue to do so today.

To Tom Newkirk, Matt Glover, Kathy Collins, Katie Wood Ray, Kristi Mraz, Christine Hertz, Maggie Roberts, Kate Roberts, Pernille Ripp, Chad Everett, Dr. Dana Stachowiak, and Kelly Gallagher, for writing, speaking and teaching like total bosses.

To the entire Boothbay, #BBLit17 village who made the space possible to tell my father's story for the first time. Special shoutouts to Kylene Beers, Bob Probst, Linda Rief, Teri Lesesne, and Penny Kittle. You all became family that week.

To the entire #HFellows squad and Ellin Keene who put important conversations first. Spotlight on Cornelius Minor (my eduBatman) and Dr. Sonja Cherry-Paul (my model for life) for holding up a mirror and handing me a clearer lens. You guys are the Real MVPs.

To my mentor *Smokey Daniels*, where do I begin? 2009. I often say it was the education version of having Justin Timberlake walk through your classroom door. Smokey quips that he was just trying to "bring sexy back." That's an old road joke of ours. Many authors have their Don Graves or Don Murray or Lucy Calkins. I have you, Smoke. And I won't let you or your family go. Let's get back to work, mentor. The floor of your studio is waiting to write another book.

To the artist village: Much of this book was brainstormed while I was running with a compiled playlist entitled, *You Got This*. The flow of my ideas and the disruption of my mental monotony is owed to the artists and their art. I share this in gratitude and to also pay it forward as a *Being the Change playlist* for you:

John Legend (Love me Now)■K'NAAN(Wavin' Flag)■Maria Gadú (Shimbalaié)■Kendrick Lamar (HUMBLE)■Ed Sheeran (Barcelona)■Jay Z (Ni**as in Paris)■Rich Homie Quan (Flex (ooh, ooh, ooh))■Fiona Apple (Shadow Boxer)■Paul Simon (Diamonds on the Soles of Her Shoes)■Tribe Call Quest (Can I Kick It?)■Common (Glory)■Basement Jaxx (Where's Your Head at)■Van Morrison (Crazy Love)■Justin Bieber (Love Yourself)■ OMI (Cheerleader)■Justin Timberlake (Pusher Love Girl)■Neyo■Drake■Ms. Lauryn Hill■Eminem■Beyoncé■Esperanza Spaulding■Janet Jackson■Quincy Jones■Taylor Swift■Hanson (Mmm Bop)■Erick Sermon (React)■The Wiseguys (Ooh la la)■Janelle Monáe & Miguel (Primetime)■Rihanna (Love on the Brain)■The Weeknd

(Rockin')▪Niall Horan (Slow Hands)▪Avicii (Wake Me Up)▪DJ Khaled (I'm the One)▪Matisyahu (One Day)▪Beastie Boys (So Whatchya Want). Keep creating.

To the Ahmed village: My identity web is what it is because of you. Thank you for packing tenacity, perspective and compassion into my backpack as I explore this big world. Mom, thanks for always packing the food, your love language. Alia, Zayn, Lena and Noah, you have given us spirit and laughter we didn't know was possible. I write knowing that you are part of a generation that will show us all how it's done. Samira and Asra, thanks for paving and shaping the way for me and letting me tag along (choice or no choice). To the Top6 and Bottom6, thanks for always having my back. Miss all of you guys every day.

Nathan, you have become my family. I pinched myself a little on the steps of The Met that day. Still do. Thank you for always doing inquiry in this world with me. Love and laughter have never felt so good.

Finally, Dad, thank you for always being the example of how to interact with the world; much of this book is written because of you.

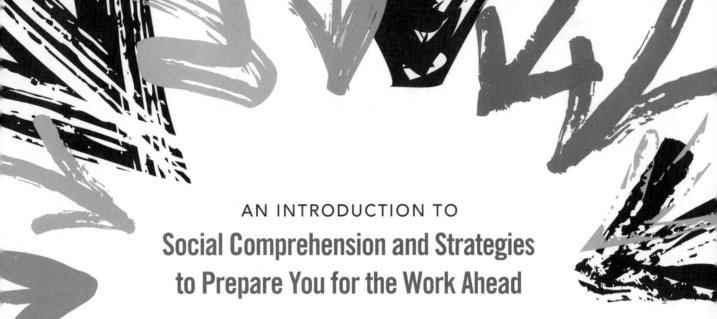

AN INTRODUCTION TO
Social Comprehension and Strategies to Prepare You for the Work Ahead

I'm sitting with a group of sixth graders in a public elementary school in Chicago. The kids are speaking.

> *"We have a lot of friends that are Mexican. We don't want a wall."*

> *"My own family won't be able to come here if they ban Muslims."*

> *"We are scared of some of the things we hear on TV."*

> *"Our parents turn the TV off if there is any type of news on. They don't want us hearing all of the bad stuff."*

> *"Why can't we talk about the real stuff in school?"*

Down the hall, three kids have just finished reading Jeanette Winter's *The Librarian of Basra*, which brought up some current connections for them.

> *"I am confused. Why would anyone bomb a school, hospital, or library?"*

> *"We play soccer together, our Mexican friends, all of us. We don't want a big wall between the US and Mexico or a war."*

> *"Even my family—they can't come here. They will be banned from coming to America [because they are Muslim]."*

I'm meeting with a small group of fourth graders in a private independent school on the Upper East Side of New York City. I hear that some of the second graders have been mirroring the political rhetoric they have been hearing, telling classmates, "You're gonna get sent back and your family is gonna have to pay for the wall!" The fourth graders ask me in a very direct manner whom I am voting for in the upcoming election. And when I try and take the politically correct (neutral) route that is usually expected of teachers, they ask again, explaining, "We are asking because we are scared. Our families identify with all the groups of people who are being targeted."

I'm sure that you have stories of your own to tell about situations or conversations that have sprung up at school, perhaps leaving you caught off guard and even a little uncomfortable. It might be political rhetoric that rippled through your classroom. It might be that moment when you felt the room become icy after someone made an offensive comment. It might be a daily barrage of comments that label, disparage, or even attack others. It might be the dry spot you feel in the back of your throat when you consider how to address news of a death, a shooting, or a terrorist attack.

In this book, we'll work together to address these moments during, after, and most important, before they arise. Not with silence, or glossing over, or punishment. Instead, we will give ourselves permission to create learning conditions where kids can ask the questions they want to ask, muddle through how to say the things they are thinking, and have tough conversations. We will be proactive in this pursuit. Truthfully, we will not have all the answers. No one does. So we will do the best with what we do have and then work to be better. We have the tools to facilitate conversations and address questions that are brought up abruptly or that come trickling in from the hallways. We have experiences and identities that bring great bias, whether explicit or implicit; whether we feel it tugging at our thoughts or don't even realize it's there until we find ourselves blurting out something unexpected. We understand the world through our own hearts and our minds' eyes. And because we can't always comprehend human behavior, especially of people we don't know personally, we will be curious and open-minded to what it is that we don't know. We will model this for our students; we will practice it in our staff meetings and in our daily lives as people who have a profound effect on generations of human beings.

Without this space for dialogue and questions, or this reassurance that we will listen, we send the message to kids that they must keep carrying on. That they must keep their hearts buried by a flurry of stereotypes, media-generated hype, and tragic events. That they must keep their heads down. Blinders on. That they must work harder toward personal happiness and success without considering the effects we have on others in our world.

Because, frighteningly enough, that seems to be the message they're hearing from us.

What Are We Teaching Kids About Empathy?

In 2014, the Harvard Graduate School of Education's Making Caring Common Project labeled our youth's values as "awry" in a study entitled *The Children We Mean to Raise: The Real Messages Adults Are Sending About Values*. The report promptly points the finger at adults as the source of this generation's muddled composition: "Our youth's values appear to be awry, and the messages that adults are sending may be at the heart of the problem." The project surveyed ten thousand middle and high school students in thirty-three schools (twenty-one traditional public, seven charter, and five independent schools over ten years). Here is the main query posed to students:

Rank what is most important to you:

1. Achieving at a high level

2. Happiness (feeling good most of the time)

3. Caring for others

The major finding was that many of our kids today (of diverse representation) define personal success through achievement and happiness rather than concern for others. Over 80 percent of youth ranked high achievement or happiness as their top choice. I know you just did the math; that leaves about two thousand out of ten thousand who chose caring for others. In response to another query, students ranked hard work well above fairness. When asked to make their thinking visible for the researchers some were very clear in their greater outlook on life: "If you are not happy, life is nothing. After that, you want to do well. And after that, expend any excess energy on others."

So, where are kids getting the message of ambivalence toward others?

As Harvey "Smokey" Daniels has been heard saying to groups of educators, we have to stop blaming the kids: for not reading, for not being collaborative, for not being kind to one another. Kids mirror the language and behaviors adults exhibit. So it is up to the adults in their lives to model compassion for them. We have to take it head on. I consider it to be a responsibility.

Currently, compassion is not in the arterial system of education. It is in our national (often reactionary) rhetoric, but not in our national standards and certainly not in the tests that we are tethered to. And it is in our national branding. *Compassion* flies proudly on school banners in atriums and foyers. It is wordsmithed into vision and mission statements on learning institutions' websites. But with escalating demands on kids and teachers and the demoralization of the teaching profession, kindness, compassion, and empathy become only buzzwords on posters we pass by on our way to deliver the next high-achieving kid into the same system.

I've heard wise educators say that the health of a school depends on the number of elephants in the room. When we don't think we are responsible for helping kids address the issues that they say matter, when we confine discussions of those issues to fictional characters in literature, or when we try to control the discourse ourselves, these issues surface in behavior, in misunderstandings, in mistreatment, in cruelty, in self-doubt, and even in violence. Is it then right to point the finger at the kids? Bryan Stevenson, social justice advocate and founder of the Equal Justice Initiative, often speaks of the importance of "getting close to things that matter," arguing that we cannot make real change from a distance (2015). Replace the word *school* in the first sentence of this paragraph with *neighborhood, community, organization, system, office,* or *team,* and the same holds true. We can begin to address the elephants in our society by having open, honest, sometimes difficult conversations in our classrooms. Democratic discourse matters. Our kids matter. We need to get close to both and dig in.

Linda Darling-Hammond has said, "In order to create a cohesive community and a consensus on how to proceed, school people must have the occasion to engage in democratic discourse about the real stuff of teaching and learning" (1997, 336). We are in a fortunate position: we can guide students to question and engage in critical conversations where ideas are freely exchanged. As educators and caretakers of children, we often jump in to rescue them before discussions get too sensitive. We don't always trust the kids to navigate conversations with us on the sidelines. But if we set them up for success, and build in ample lessons for them to practice strategies of social comprehension, we help them construct the strategies to champion courageous conversations when hot-button issues come to the rug.

Getting Started with Social Comprehension

The initial step in addressing the curriculum the world hands us is daunting. Societal norms and our own human tendencies of fight or flight caution us to be wary of entering a space where there is potential discomfort. *Why would I engage in a discussion where feelings can be hurt? Are my kids ready for this? How do I take time from what I need to "cover" to do this?* And, of course, *Why would I rock the boat when everything is just fine?*

The truth, of course, is that while there can be much to be thankful for, everything is not always just fine.

It is imperative in a democracy that many voices *are* included in discourse, and conversations around relevant topics are not easy when it comes to negotiating everyone's individual experiences. Avoiding these conversations now—at a point in our students' lives when they are the most able to consider new perspectives—will yield a generational ignorance we can't afford for the future. Ignorance is *not* bliss. Ignorance is a luxury of the privileged and a barrier to the unnoticed and underserved. So how do we take the first steps to engaging in vulnerable conversations where risk is high but the payoff could be even greater?

This book is based on the idea that we can develop skills and habits to help us comprehend social issues and participate in relevant, transparent conversations. Social comprehension, like academic comprehension, is how we make meaning from and mediate our relationship with the world. We understand that the meaning making, or socialization, is learned, not inherited. Each chapter in this book includes lessons and/or practical help for students to learn and engage in a targeted social comprehension concept. Our thinking will change often as we practice being more socially literate citizens of the world, so we allow for and model the same for our students as we construct comprehension and cultivate our empathy together. The "At First I Thought . . . Now I Think" journal page in this introduction gives you and your students a tool to reflect on how the experiences in the lessons are affecting your outlook. In the work of social comprehension, we want to be as transparent as possible and make our thinking visible.

The final chapter of the book addresses how we, as educators, can help children make sense of the news they bring to school and the curriculum the world keeps handing them. We must have a strong foundation of social comprehension in place. If we can commit to approaching this work as the lead learner, teaching with curiosity and modeling vulnerability rather than rigid certainty, we can build habitats of trust where kids (and adults) participate in a learning discussion, and where expression, identity, and social literacy matter.

A Few Guiding Principles

The methods we use to ensure peaceful classrooms often involve avoiding difficult conversations or controversial topics. However, if we want kids to learn to comprehend others' identities and perspectives, those identities and perspectives must be shared. To do this productively while also maintaining a safe—if not conflict-free—environment for our kids, we may need to modify our approach. Here are a few general guidelines as you begin.

Do the Work Yourself First—and Often

I recommend experiencing the lessons in this book first not with your students, but with your peers. This examination is just as valuable for adults as it is for kids: I have used the core elements of these lessons with adults in professional development sessions for years.

More importantly, if we want to teach students to be compassionate, complex thinkers, we must first muddle through this work ourselves. Otherwise we may not be prepared for the outcomes: the fight or flight, the tears, the crawling of skin, the desire to shake the tables. As Robert L. Fried writes in *The Passionate Teacher*, "Any of us, when we're nervous or when things threaten to get out of control, is likely to revert to a more controlling or defensive posture" (2001, 150). Rather than retreating to control or going on the defense, we have to dig deep. The more we are able to be introspective upfront, the more comfortable we may become with the *discomfort* of powerful discussions that can move all of us to new levels as learners and critical thinkers, and to sometimes Herculean feats of humility.

In my experience, the best way to take on this work is in a group. Try a gradual build starting with pairs, then small groups, then large groups, establishing norms for discussion as the number of voices grows. It is with others that we learn to listen; as we hear new ideas and points of view, we grow in understanding. W. Kamau Bell says, "I believe in the power of awkward conversations to initiate change. When we can talk with and laugh with (instead of at) each other, then we can slowly figure out ways to make more room for each other's humanity." If your own discomfort is too great, read through the suggestions in this chapter on your own until you're comfortable diving in with others. Keep in mind that we are asking kids to turn and talk constantly. To solve what we think needs solving, to be the change we wish to see, we have to engage in this talk too.

Keep the Focus on the Kids, Not on You

Remembering that the focus is not just about you gives you permission to take the pressure off yourself. When we try to empathize by constantly relaying our own experience, we can stop others from sharing, and we miss the opportunity to learn wholly about their experiences. We don't fully listen. Picture this situation: news walks into our classrooms—perhaps a pet dying, the loss of a family member, or world news. Immediately, we try to think of ways to connect. But when our empathy statements begin with "I," kids may roll their eyes in anticipation: "Oh man, here comes another story about *her*." Our lives as educators are full of rich and diverse experiences, but we cannot possibly have an understanding of every hand that has been dealt to our students. And if a comment arises in class that offends our personal belief system and we fall into the trap of responding ourselves rather than allowing students' truths to be expressed, we are controlling the ownership of the learning. Keeping this general questioning principle in mind can help: What does this mean for *you*? Not, what does this mean for *me*? Your strongest superpower in the classroom is kid watching. Make it about what the kids are doing and saying. That is, listen; don't just wait to talk.

Consider How You See Your Kids

How well do you know your students? Researcher and visionary teacher Don Graves (2006) posited that adults should not attempt to teach children anything until they know at least ten things about each child as a person—that a certain girl loves chocolate-chip cookies, for example, or that one boy's dog means the world to him. When you think about your students, are you seeing them as they would define themselves, or in the terms we often use to describe kids: *struggling reader, low at math, hyper, talkative*? Are we saying, "Sara wants to be known as someone who is an avid reader of mystery books," or "Sara only reads mystery books." There is a difference. The following challenges come from Don Graves:

> *Challenge 1:* Visualize one student in your past or current experience. Consider the ten things that you know about this child as a person. How easy or challenging might it be to do that for your entire roster? Next to each child's name, keep a running list of the ten things that they share with you about themselves. Not the ten things you assume about them, but the pieces of themselves they trust you with.

> *Challenge 2:* Try seeing and then describing your students using only nouns and verbs, not adjectives. Make a three-column chart with "Students' Names," "Nouns," and "Verbs" as the column headings. Use your roster to help you do this. Graves went student by student and committed himself to dedicating more time to those he found difficult to visualize in this way. Consider how your language positions students. Do you see a student as "disruptive", or do you notice that she *carries* a *soccer ball* to school every day, reenacting game highlights and moves every chance she gets? Pay close attention and be candid in how you are kid watching in your classroom, and that will inform the language you use when you discuss, address,

and view your students. What are the things they carry? What are the things they do? Full of our own bias, we can anticipate that students will behave one way, or we can watch how they express themselves in telling their story to us.

Once you try these challenges, you'll soon see how easy it is for judgment to creep into the ways we describe others. You will also be able to come up with what I call inquiry lifesavers: books, news, anecdotes, and other now-personal connections you can share with a student because you put in the time to see them for who they really are. The lessons in Chapter 1 will also give you opportunities to understand how students see themselves.

Be OK with Silence and Discomfort (aka, Don't "Save" Every Moment)

We don't need to be the sole saviors when kids experience moments of tension or sensitivity in class. This can mean letting a student's emotionally charged words hang in the air without instantly jumping in to smooth things over. It might mean waiting in roaring silence while students decide how to respond to one another without your deciding for them. Letting students know that you can wait a long time allows them to become comfortable with the discomfort of silence. There is so much growth in this space.

I realize this strategy might sound counterintuitive at first. Aren't we the ones trying to make a safe place for our kids? Silence makes us uneasy, especially in a room charged with tension, anger, or other emotions. However, people can weather anxiety if they feel that they are in a safe situation. The work you'll do with students to value their identities (outlined in the early lessons of this book) will help to create that safe space.

In fact, I have found in the toughest situations, the hardest conversations, it is always other kids, not me, who know exactly what to say to a friend who is struggling. Kids have that acute sense of justice and a big heart to boot. In strong communities, they know when to lend a hand, a shoulder, or a story that connects them to a friend in need. When we learn to accept that discomfort is part of learning, when we avoid responding out of our own anxiety, we give students opportunities to take the lead.

Decenter Your Normal

Visualize a day in your life: from your home to school, school to extracurricular activities and evening commitments, activities to daily errands around your town, and then back to your neighborhood. See the faces, the physical abilities, the familiar structures, the socioeconomic status of those around you. Are they similar to you or different—not only in race or ethnicity, but in diversity of thought, customs, ability? Now, what if you visualized a person you perceived as an outlier and then thought about *their* experience in *your* normal day?

We see the world through the lens of our own experience. We normalize it and don't question the structures and systems that allow some to feel safe (and others marginalized)—we don't go to that grocery store on the other side of town or send our kids to the parks, pools, or schools on the other side of the tracks. We have to actively work to realize how we center one race, familial structure, gender identification, degree of ableism, religion, name, or love relationship. We need to pay attention to the language we use and how it can position people, customs, food, or traditions outside of what we view to be normal (the center)—for instance, the way we describe skin tone or hair (*exotic*) or the way we label foods (*smelly, weird, gross*). That language keeps us at the center of what we believe is expected and therefore socially acceptable. This is not easy, as we naturally are at the center of our own universe. (There is even a lesson on this later in this book.) But we don't have license to certify *normal*. That is a basic tenet in the work of social comprehension. While *diversity* is the word of the day, when we decenter the dominant, normative narratives in society we make way for not only diversity, but also inclusion. As you do this work, decenter yourself and sideline your own discomfort in order to make way for the voices, emotions, and experiences of others, especially your students.

Enter with Humility

"We all live in a culture of Tell and find it difficult to ask, especially to ask in a humble way," writes Edgar H. Schein in *Humble Inquiry* (2014). Schein's observation that our culture values *knowing* over messy learning is evident in the way we revere experts and correct answers. More subtly, our "culture of Tell" is also a factor in our own biases, which "tell" about others' experiences without consulting the people they describe. When we feel comfortable being an expert, we may be less able to hear other ideas and perspectives. To be fully open to understanding the experiences of others, we must be willing to *not* be experts. Instead, we should practice being learners who enter conversations with humility and ask questions when we don't understand.

Everyone makes meaning of the information the world has given them in their own individual way. We interpret differently. We draw different conclusions. We will not see eye to eye.

And that is OK.

Rather than battling with another person's conclusions, we can go back to what we *don't* already know: back to the beginnings, to the middles of stories, and examine how the endings concluded where they did. In this intentional exposure and reflection there is growth. We learn as much as we can and we leave with more questions than answers. If we enter with humility, with the desire to understand, we will hear the whole stories first, before we judge the endings.

Remember That Progress Takes Time, Effort, and Heart Work

In the real world, this work is incremental. It is not punctuated by instantaneous turnarounds or by Hollywood-style climaxes or endings. Social comprehension is a constant recalibration of one's relation with the self and with others. We may notice our own growth—that we are gradually letting go of our desire to be "right," or finding ways to listen to others in our community and understand why they respond the way they do. We may end up with more questions than we started with. We will also carry the weight of the moments when we're not able to do all that we'd hoped. So we rest, reflect, and get back to work. There are no quick fixes for long-term progress. Some of the suggested actions in this book may be daunting or make you wonder if you're up for the challenge. The answer is yes, you are—but it will take time and lots of heart work. We have great capability as individuals, classrooms, communities, and as nations to progress forward if we have the will to do the work.

Cultivate Your Compassion

These lessons are all entry points to a bigger process. My high school humanities teacher, Mrs. Flannigan, used to always remind us to "cultivate your gardens." "You get to grow your own garden in life," she would say. "You decide to keep or get rid of the weeds, see and nurture the beautiful pieces of it. But it is up to you what grows." She would help by opening up our eyes to new and diverse voices in art, music, literature, science, and the systems of our history. We would talk, debate, give speeches on the truths of others, write, read, and eventually express our own truths.

Mrs. Flannigan was ahead of her time. Today, psychologists believe that sociability and the complexities of human relationships, with empathy at the core, drive human evolution (Hanson 2010). We have to get proximate: read, write, speak, listen, negotiate, and bridge the distance between our world and others'. We cannot simply lean on our tweets about one book on diversity and then fly the empathy flag. We have to grow empathy in all aspects of our lives: notice all the small decisions we make each day, be aware of our bias and actively work against it. And we need to continue to evolve as individuals and as a society. After all these years, I hear Ms. Flannigan. We have to cultivate our gardens. We need to do the work of social comprehension.

Tracking Growth Across the Year

Once you have worked through one or more of the lessons in this book with students, introduce them to the "At First I Thought . . . Now I Think" journal sheet, a simple T-chart that educators have been using for years across content areas. Ask them to note places where they've felt their views or understandings shift.

We have been doing a lot of thinking and grappling, questioning and revealing during these lessons. When we work as hard we have, it is really important to reflect. This is the reason why your coaches talk to you after practices, games, and recitals and ask, "How do you think that went?"

I have some journal pages that I think would help us to see how far we have come in being a little more self-aware. We could think about it this way: What do you know about yourself now that you didn't just a few weeks ago? What you know now may come from asking questions at home, from a conversation you had with a peer or with me. It could come from the writing you did, an idea that came to you . . . anything.

And then once you think about yourself, it may be good to consider how we may view others differently: What did you learn that is new about someone else? How did that change how you view them? These are personal pages for your eyes and mine when we talk. You get to choose how you share them outside of that, but I will never cold call on you to share what changes you have made.

Make this journal sheet available to your students periodically, giving them additional pages as necessary, so that they can read what they've written in the past, reflect on the heart work they have been doing, and consider their collaborations with classmates. You'll find a reminder to direct students back to this journal page at the end of each set of lessons. The kids can continue their work on additional copies of the chart, building a journal they keep with them as their experiences grow. In the past, students have asked to tape the pages into their notebooks for a more authentic diary or scrapbook feel. I have observed many of my students using these journals as a reference during group discussions. The goal in returning to this sheet across the year is, first, to help students to see and track changes in their thinking over time. Second, by revisiting the journal page at multiple points during the year, we can help to make the simple, yet powerful practice of reflecting on new learning and self-discovery part of students' personal tools for social comprehension.

Figure I.1: An example of "At First I Thought . . . Now I Think" in action

Before a social comprehension lesson, Reid, a fourth-grade teacher, asked his students to answer the question, "What makes up a family?" in the left column of their chart. Then, after the lesson, they revisited their notes and responded to the same prompt again in the right column. Notice how students' thinking changed.

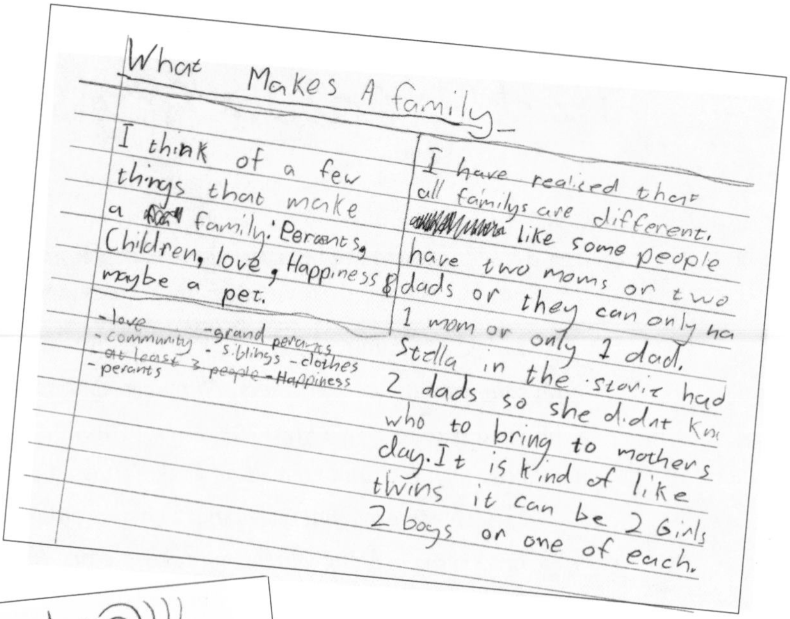

What Makes A family

| I think of a few things that make a family. Perents, Children, love, Happiness & maybe a pet. | I have realized that all familys are different, like some people have two moms or two dads or they can only ha 1 mom or only 1 dad. Stella in the storie had 2 dads so she didnt know who to bring to mothers day. It is kind of like twins it can be 2 Girls or one of each. |

- love   -grand perants
- community -siblings -clothes
- at least 3 people -Happiness
- perants

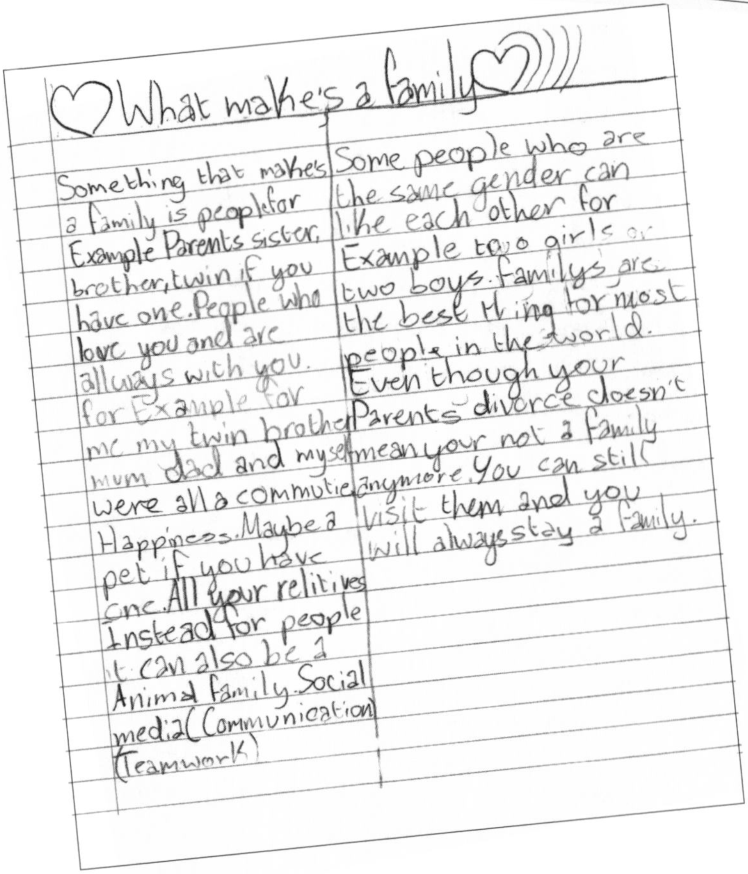

♡ What make's a family ♡

| Something that make's a family is people for Example Parents sister, brother, twin if you have one. People who love you and are allways with you. for Example for me my twin brother mum dad and myself were all a commutie. Happiness. Maybe a pet if you have one. All your relitives Instead for people it can also be a Animal family. Social media(Communication) (Teamwork) | Some people who are the same gender can like each other for Example two girls or two boys. familys are the best thing for most people in the world. Even though your Parents divorce doesn't mean your not a family anymore. You can still visit them and you will always stay a family. |

At First I Thought . . .	Now I Think . . .

1

Exploring Our Identities

I am in the hot seat in front of a group of curious fifth graders at NIST International School in Bangkok. All eyes are on me, the guest, the foreigner. I have about fifteen minutes with them just to introduce myself as I tour the school, and so I do what any person looking to engage in full disclosure with nine-year-olds would do. I say, "I'm going to share my top three things I think you should know about me and my identity and then you can ask me any question you want." I take a deep breath. "So, something you should know about me is I *love* soccer."

The kids had already been making nonverbal connections to me by way of smiling, but now I saw what I call "OMG faces."

"Do you mean, football?" one calls out.

"Yes! Football! Sorry, I forgot everywhere else in the world calls it that. Something else you should know about me is that I have two nieces and two nephews whom I adore." I pause a moment.

"And the last thing is, I am a teacher in America."

I look at the kids and smile.

"OK, your turn."

Their hands shoot up.

"Where do you come from?"

"America."

A young lady follows up: "No, like, where do you come from, like your family?"

"Well, I live in New York, but I was born in Chicago, which is also in America. But my parents are from India, if that is what you are asking."

The young lady lights up. "I am from India too."

Two more call out, "Yeah, me too."

I field a few more questions about who my favorite "footballer" is and some connections from kids who have traveled to New York or anywhere in America where they have family.

After we finish our discussion, my new friend "from India too" comes up to me and wants to know more about me, my family, and India. She is super excited to share when I ask her a couple questions about her ancestry. She lingers. And I get it. Even though our ties are to different regions in India and probably to different religions, subcultures, and customs, she can see herself in me (and I in her), and that is what mattered most in that moment. To both of us. We felt heard. We felt understood. We felt visible.

The kids are our curriculum

We have an obligation to make kids feel visible. When we recognize and value students' identities, we make time and space for them in the daily classroom routines, curriculum, and dialogue. We can help students shine a light on who they are: their hopes and dreams, talents, family histories, how they identify culturally, the languages they speak, how they learn best, the story of their names, what they can teach us.

How do we make kids *feel* visible? My sense of effectiveness as a teacher has always been tied to my relationships with my students. I invest time in getting to know their individual identities, find the connections we have, and learn more about them by asking questions. I have informal conversations with them on the peripheries: walking in the halls, recess, lunch, sports practice. I do a lot of kid watching noticing their "flight patterns" in class and around the school. As educators, the advice we often hear about forming relationships with students—don't be "friends" with students, get too personal, blur the lines, or smile the first couple weeks—builds a dangerous wall between us and our kids. If my goal as an educator is to create an environment that fosters humanity, I have to genuinely work to build, bridge, and bolster relationships in my community. Relationships are essential to teaching and learning because teaching and learning are social endeavors. We need to love our students the way Sonia Nieto (2009, 94) implores us to do in her canon of research and practice: "Caring and love are more than just sentimental or superficial affection. . . . Instead, caring and love are about just the opposite, that is, having high expectations and great hopes for all students, believing in their abilities, and respecting their identities."

The lessons in this chapter are a purposeful way to begin with the kids—*they are our curriculum*. Everything we do can be planned and scaffolded from our initial rapport-building activities and dialogue with our students. Consider, for example: What activities do I plan for opening week, the start of the year? Are these the same activities that they do year after year with every teacher? Why do I choose them? Do I read and respond to this initial student work? Do I pore over them and make observations? Do I just file away the kids' work? Hang it up, write "Super!" on it and then hand it back to them? What will I do with all the identity data I gather?

Some of my personal goals for these opening experiences are for the students to:

- engage in self-identifying and self-reflection

- honor their own families, cultures, and language

- negotiate their identities in this world

- connect and wonder about the identities of others

- affirm who they are

- speak their truths and accept what others say as their truth

- co-construct what it looks and feels like to share the planet with other human beings

. . . and for me to do my best listening so I can tailor the learning experience for them.

As my mentor, Smokey Daniels, says, a commitment to knowing and caring about a person's identity is "the road to empathy." When we give our students the floor to say who they are and what that means to them, they are far less likely to allow someone to do it for them.

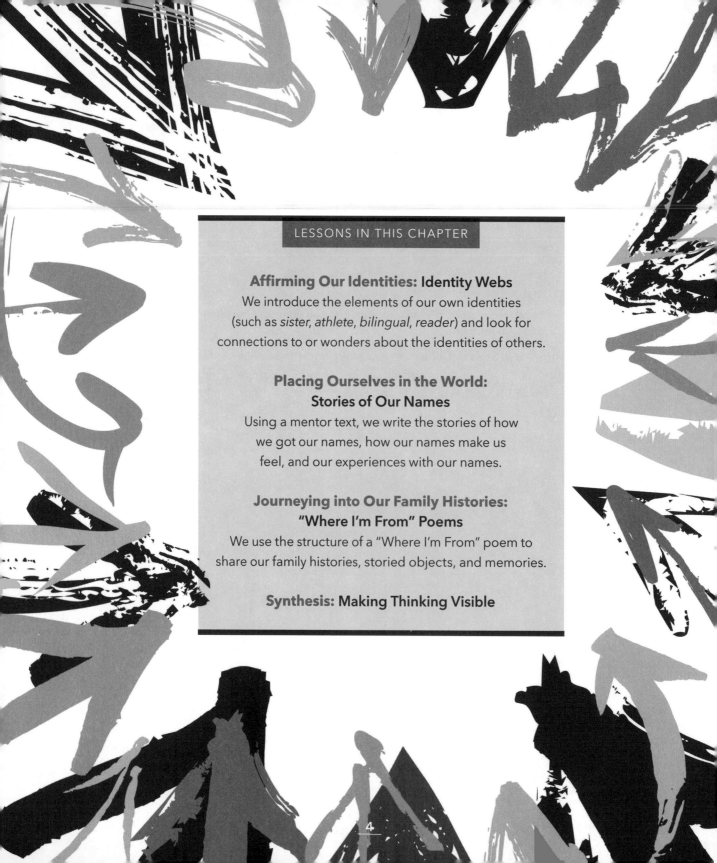

Affirming Our Identities

Identity Webs

What Are Identity Webs?

Identity webs are personalized graphic tools that help us consider the many factors that shape who we are.

Why Use Identity Webs?

Self-exploration is not always an easy topic to approach. I first explored identity webs at a Facing History and Ourselves workshop as an introductory lens to how you view and define yourself, in roles you are confident in claiming and sharing: a teacher, a parent, a

reader, a runner, a knitter, a traveler. Once named, these become an entry point to initiating conversation with others. It is a beautiful beginning-of-the-year lesson, but more than an icebreaker. Identity webs help us find commonalities which springboard us to notice, wonder, and see the humanity in one another. What matters is not the web itself, but the dialogue that it makes possible and how that dialogue is a catalyst for rapport building.

When Could Identity Webs Be Used?

- When introducing yourself to your students.
- When working to connect with your students as well as help them connect with one another.
- When reading about a protagonist or actor in history, with each student creating a web for the person as the class learns more.
- When working to build understanding of and empathy for a particular individual or group of people with whom students may have little background knowledge.

Identity webs can be done on loose paper or in journals. I use them as an opening activity on the first day of school and revisit them many times a year. While you may choose to display them in the classroom, they are not meant to be decorative wallpaper. They become documents we revisit, reference, and revise over and over as we learn together across the year.

STEP 1: CHOOSE AN ENGAGING TEXT TO READ WITH YOUR CLASS
On the first day of school, have kids come to the community meeting area right away and bring along a pencil and a notebook. Start with a shared read-aloud to help calm the nerves and focus the energy this initial meeting brings. Beginning with a read-aloud also sends the message that reading aloud, reading together, and reading picture books is something the class will do. It is cool and accepted in this room.

Choose a text where the identity of the protagonist is named and inferred through the written language or images. Short, high-interest, biography picture books work well. I recommend reading the text yourself and creating an identity web for the person so you can see if it will work well with your students.

Suggested Stack for Exploring Our Own Identities

Picture Books

Ada Twist, Scientist; Rosie Revere, Engineer; and *Iggy Peck, Architect* by Andrea Beaty

Amelia and Eleanor Go for a Ride by Pam Munoz Ryan

Emmanuel's Dream: The True Story of Emmanuel Ofosu Yeboah by Laurie Ann Thompson

Harvesting Hope: The Story of Cesar Chavez by Kathleen Krull

Jacob's New Dress by Sarah and Ian Hoffman

Malala, a Brave Girl from Pakistan and *Iqbal, a Brave Boy from Pakistan: Two Stories of Bravery* by Jeanette Winter

Manfish: A Story of Jacques Cousteau by Jennifer Berne

Stella Brings the Family by Miriam Schiffer

Sunday Chutney by Aaron Blabey

The Librarian of Basra by Jeanette Winter

The Youngest Marcher by Cynthia Levinson

Poetry

Bravo! Poems About Amazing Hispanics by Margarita Engle

Out of Wonder: Poems Celebrating Poets by Kwame Alexander
with Chris Colderley and Marjory Wentworth

Still I Rise by Maya Angelou

Essay

"Little Things Are Big" by Jesus Colon

"Orientation Day" by Jennifer Wang

Short Story Anthologies

America Street: A Multicultural Anthology of Stories edited by Anne Mazer

First Crossings: Stories About Teen Immigrants by Donald R. Gallo

Flying Lessons edited by Ellen Oh

The Paper Menagerie and Other Stories by Ken Liu (particularly the title story)

When I Was Your Age: Original Stories About Growing Up, Volumes I and II,
edited by Amy Ehrlich

STEP 2: INVITE STUDENTS TO THINK, WRITE, PAIR, SHARE

Because it is so early in the year, we want kids to have a little breathing room before we push them into talks with new peers. First I give them a direction that ignites their personal schema:

> *We are going to kick off the year with an idea that we will revisit tons: identity. I want you to stop and think for a minute: What comes to mind when you hear or see the word identity?* (I always write it on the board for all learners.) *Use that inner voice first, the voice that is bringing all of your prior experience to the front of your mind. Then, write your ideas.*

Everyone has a shiny, clean, new notebook and a pencil they are excited about using (and that they have not yet lost) on the first day, so writing is welcomed. The hands of some of your ready-to-share-anywhere learners will go up right away (a great formative assessment of who is ready to share in whole-group work). Remind them to just give everyone some thinking time. Then have them share with a partner:

Thanks for putting your thinking on paper. I think we can get smarter together on this one, so I am going to ask that in a minute—when I say "go!"—you turn to a partner near you and share what you wrote down. Think about what has to happen for that to work: you need to notice and identify who is near you, be aware of who is included and who isn't, and maybe even say hi before you engage. Think you can handle it? (Here, I am really looking for the kids who are observing whether everyone has a partner.) *You'll know it is time to come back together when I say 3, 2, 1 . . . OK? Go!*

Try leaning into the pairs, looking for two things: One, did the kids have enough time to write some thoughts on identity? Two, how are they doing as they talk? Are they sharing airtime with their partners? Being active listeners (making eye contact, asking for clarification, writing down what their partner wrote as a form of celebrating their thinking)? You may want to record social behaviors to inform your instruction: all of the behaviors of active listening can be taught in mini-lessons. You may also find yourself jumping in to listen, talk, smile, and greet them again on this first day. Give them about thirty seconds to a minute depending on the energy. Bring them back with a *3, 2, 1*, noticing how they come back together.

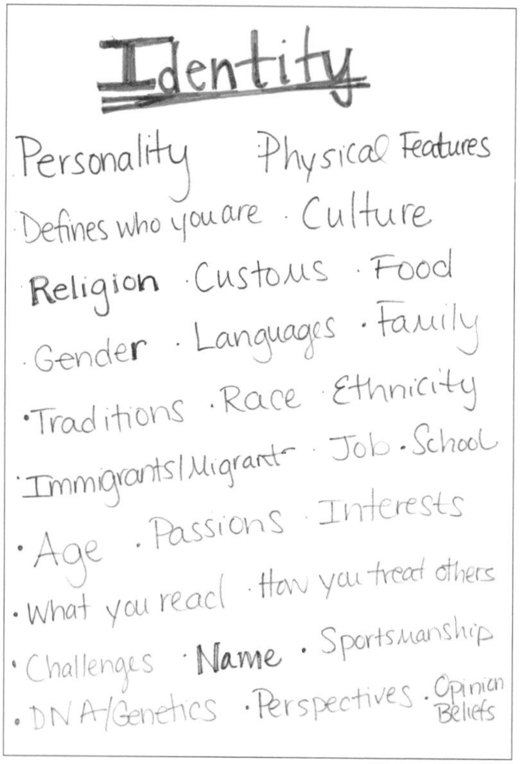

Figure 1.1 A kid-generated list from a middle-school class.

OK, you have thought on your own, written down your thinking, and gotten smarter with a partner. Let's hear from some partnerships on your conversation. What does identity mean to you or to you and your partner?

By now, I typically find that a few more kids than before raise their hands. This is a direct result of the self-confidence they have built in their conversations with their peers. As the kids talk, scribe their contributions on an anchor chart labeled "Identity." Invite them to do the same in their journals.

One idea will lead to another. Honor the kids' responses by adding them to the chart, but don't worry about trying to form an exhaustive list at this point. Once the initial flurry of ideas is over, you can keep the momentum of the lesson going during the read-aloud by asking kids to suggest more items for the chart as the story uncovers them. For example, if age doesn't show up on our chart at first, it may come up in the story. This is a working document and a definition that you will build together.

STEP 3: MODEL AN IDENTITY WEB DURING READ-ALOUD

When introducing the read-aloud, prime kids with the idea that you are going to look into the *identity* of this character. Let them know that you are going to create something called a web in order to map the identity of the character. Ask them to follow your lead as you draw a circle and write the name of the character in the middle.

> *Can you guys follow my lead and draw this circle in your notebook right after that list of identity characteristics we just built together? Write the character's name in the middle. As we read, we are going to investigate any clues the author gives us into the identity of _____.*
>
> *I will do the first couple for you and I'll look to you to help me as well.*

Begin reading. There is usually one helpfully glaring piece of identity introduced in the first page(s) of these texts that gives you a little teaching alley-oop. Think aloud for the kids and add this bit to the web. After you do this one or two more times, the kids usually begin noticing on their own, so you can gradually release the bulk of the work over to them. Stop a couple times during the reading to have them turn and talk, sharing what they have as you grow the web together. Finish the book and check in one last time.

STEP 4: ESTABLISHING RAPPORT: KIDS MAKE THEIR OWN IDENTITY WEBS

To transition kids into making their own webs, first model the start of your own. Look to the shared web you just created as a jumping-off point.

> *There are so many things on this web that we were able to glean from this story. We were able to have a deeper look into this character's identity by creating this together. Now I want to turn our focus to ourselves.*

Begin your own identity web on new chart paper or by using the document camera. I begin with a think-aloud, listing various pieces of my identity that I know the kids will find a connection to as I go: soccer player, reader, sister. This is a moment of initial rapport building that also requires a little vulnerability for us as teachers as we open ourselves up to them. I promise you, a little self-disclosure goes a long way. If there are apparent connections to the web you and the class just made, look for those and think aloud. This models how the class will later build identity connections and practice asking personal questions.

Kids will naturally hunt for connections to their own lives in your web, and they'll undoubtedly have questions as well. You might ask, "Does anyone have a connection to me? Do you see something in my web you may include in yours as well?" As kids make connections, remember that these are personal associations, not answers to be graded as correct or incorrect. It's OK to let yourself respond as you would in a social situation. Let your teacher guard down and humanize the moment—ask them a follow-up question to deepen the connection, smile, or say, "Wow, I can't wait to talk to you about that later!" Your responses are a model for how students might respond to one another when they answer others' questions later in the lesson.

If you are not comfortable with a particular question, say so. For example, I might say, "Thanks for being brave by asking that question. While it is important enough to include on my web, I am still figuring out how to talk about it. Can you be my person when I am ready?" Then I give that student another opportunity to find something else they are curious about. When you model this kind of response as positive yet honest, with respectful language that students can mirror later, you help kids let go of apprehensions they might have about asking questions. Try your best not to censor your web by deliberately omitting things you're uncomfortable sharing. This is an initial practice in sharing our whole vulnerable selves. We first have to get uncomfortable before we can become comfortable in difficult conversations.

Give kids guidance about how to frame their connections and questions in the same respectful way you'll expect them to converse with one another:

As you look at my web, what are you wondering about me or things I wrote down? You might ask something like, What position did you play in soccer? or What is your favorite book of all time? or How many brothers or sisters do you have?

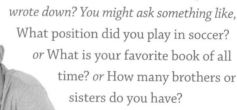

Of course, you might also have questions that are more personal. In our class, we'll be talking a lot about our identities, so it's important that we know how to respect what each of us is willing to talk about. So, if you have

a personal question, you might phrase it this way: Are you comfortable answering a question about your parents, Ms. Ahmed? *And, if I say I am, you can follow up with the question. So, what questions do you have?*

Finally, give kids the green light to try their own webs:

You have had a lot of practice reading and creating webs to have a deeper sense of what identity means to people. Now it is your turn. I would love you to go back to your seats and try your own webs. Turn back to the example from our story, the web from me, and the chart we made together if you feel stuck.

STEP 5: INDEPENDENT CREATING

This is the perfect time to move about the room and mingle with students one-on-one. Take time to notice what they are creating, where they are starting in terms of their identity, if they are relating to the character, if they are relating to you. Briefly confer with individual students, making connections and asking some questions just as you modeled with your own web. Take advantage of opportunities to build connections in these one-on-one moments. If the kids are working silently, invite them to turn and talk to share with their peers.

Figure 1.2 Simran, a rising senior, gives a glimpse not only of her interests and heritage, but also her passions, her anxieties, and her hopes and dreams. In a quick conference, I might look for a connection between us by asking about her love of travel or of the *Hamilton* play soundtrack, and I will keep in

mind some of the other things she's shared—her bravery in her transparency, her descriptions of herself as an "overthinker," and her curiosity "about everything"—as I get to know her over the year. I will look for entry points to ask her questions (Tell me more about what makes you a "hands-on learner") and I will use her responses to think about books I can recommend to her ("love a good book") and pieces of writing she can launch from here ("officially British, Kiwi at heart"). Today, I smile when I look at Simran's web because I can hear her voice in it—"frizzy hair . . . do care."

Figure 1.3 Pun, a fourth grader, chose a more visual route in sharing his identity. This tells me something right away about his preferred choice for communicating with the world and his talent! As Pun is working I am realizing I don't have a ton of connections with him (aside from soccer), so I look for opportunities to talk to him about what I am wondering. I am interested in talking to him more about his musical identity: Does he play both the piano and guitar? Does he have a preference? As someone who hasn't really touched a console since Super Nintendo and the original PlayStation myself, I wonder about his gaming: How are games different when played on all of these systems?

STEP 6: SHARING IDEAS

Sharing can be done in pairs, in small groups, or back at the rug. Prompt kids to share a few things that they included, what matters most to them, or connections they have to you or the character. Also allow kids to ask questions of one another, reminding them of the ways people can choose to answer or not. Let kids share without too much commentary from you once you get them going. In a big group share, I have given kids the challenge afterward to find one or two people with whom they had a connection and let them know. The conversation burbles in the room, springing from comments like, "Hey, we had a connection; I have read the entire Harry Potter series twice too."

Kids may want to continue adding to their own webs, especially after a share of good ideas. Let them know they can take the webs home to design them to their hearts' desire, but they must come back! I have also used webs to create an initial home-school connection by having kids interview an adult at home to see what they might include on their web, having the adult do a web along with them, or having parents make their own during Parent Open House.

↑ FOLLOW-UP

Identity webs are always in the follow-up cycle. There are many things that can be done after they are created, but the most important one is to revisit them as a touchstone text for doing the work of social comprehension. Our identity comes with stories and experiences different from those of anyone else. Use these webs as a baseline to remind kids of the things they carry always, in meeting new people, in collaboration, in difficult conversations. They can be used for a gallery walk with their classmates, or put up for a follow-up lesson that can include leaving connections or questions on sticky notes (similar to the connections and questions they practiced with you verbally). After these lessons, webs should be kept securely in their journals where they can be easily accessed for lessons to come.

⇅ ADDRESSING TENSIONS

Identity can be messy and we have to take great care in supporting kids as they figure it out; we are right alongside them on this journey. I have provided a few tensions that have come up in my classes during this work.

1. **Students don't think they have anything to put down on their web.**

   Try this: Some students will stop at only a few words and say they are "done." We can give them a nudge by noticing what is already on their web and asking some follow-up questions. We can also notice any items they have with them, on their person. Even writing utensils and backpacks have a story. That may elicit some more writing.

2. **Students are including only surface elements of their identity.**

   Try this: During the model, be extra thoughtful about addressing some pieces of your identity that may cause some personal tension for you, or that you just aren't sure how to articulate. I may share that my parents speak another language at home (Urdu) and that I don't, but it is part of who I am: I grew up hearing it and that is how my family communicates. (Language can be an area of tension for students who use a mother tongue other than English at home.) Sharing a small struggle for you may empower them to do the same.

Placing Ourselves in the World

Stories of Our Names

What Are Name Stories?

Name stories are individuals' explanations of the personal or traditional meaning, importance, or origin of their names. Writing their own stories helps kids to see the power of their own names. Listening to others' name stories unpacks the personal history of people we will spend an entire year with.

Why Examine Names?

Names matter. Central to identity, names influence who we are and how others view us. But even more important, names carry a story—a story of the past, perhaps carried across oceans or passed down through generations. They are attached to something or someone, or created and given to us. In some cases names can have the power to alter us, to give us agency, or, as history teaches—to erase us. Enslaved people were assigned the names of their masters, a process of dehumanization with the aim of obliterating people's sense of self and identity.

The story of our name is another window into the examination of identity and the connection we can make with others.

Not all names are in our personal repertoire. Names can be cultural, religious, ancestral, or invented. Many people live day to day with the looming dread of someone mispronouncing their name in an initial meeting, mistaking it on the first day of school, or misspelling it on a Starbucks cup. For example, my colleague and good friend Niamh (pronounced *Neeve*) has spent her entire life enduring mispronunciations of her Irish/Gaelic name or correcting others when they attempt to pronounce it. It took such an emotional toll on her in elementary school that it is the first lesson she shares with kids as a school counselor today. She uses Sherman Alexie's *Thunder Boy*

Jr. as a read-aloud to begin the discussion. To hear one's name repeatedly mispronounced or misspelled is often so frustrating that people may alter the spelling or pronunciation to make it easier for others. Anglicizing, Americanizing, or simplifying names is easier for assimilation, but at what cost to the bearer of the name?

If we want kids to have a strong sense of self, we can celebrate names and the stories behind them. We can also teach kids to ask about and understand the importance of names to others.

When Is a Good Time to Celebrate Name Identity?

- When introducing yourself to your students.
- When your class list is rich in diverse names.
- When working to connect with your students as well as help them connect with one another.
- When working to build understanding of and empathy for a particular individual or group of people with whom students may have little background knowledge.
- When reading a story with names that may be new to your students.

If we want kids to have a strong sense of self, we can celebrate names and the stories behind them.

- At parent night. Having parents share the story of their child's name before you ask kids to share those stories in class introduces the context of this work. It would be helpful to prompt parents to share the story with their child if they have not already.

STEP 1: GROUNDING THE WORK IN A MENTOR TEXT

The beautiful and honest language of Sandra Cisneros in *The House on Mango Street*'s Chapter 4, "Name," gives students something they can dig into together. It begins: *In English my name means hope. In Spanish it means too many letters.*

We become aware of a few things here right at the hook of the piece: The protagonist (Esperanza) has a name of Spanish language heritage. She is aware of the meaning in English, *hope*, and you can infer that her attitude toward the Spanish spelling is less than favorable.

Having done some identity work in the previous lesson, when you are on the rug together, you can have an identity web ready to go with Esperanza's name in the middle. Open with a read-aloud of this first line. Ask students to start their own webs for Esperanza as well. Begin to read the chapter to students, making notes on the web as you think aloud about what pieces of her identity she is revealing to the reader in the first two lines.

If Cisneros' text feels too challenging, you might try a picture book that includes what you are aiming for in this lesson: the story of the protagonist's name, the protagonist's thoughts about the name, and written language that matches the age and development of your students. A few suggestions:

Chrysanthemum by Kevin Henkes

My Name is Sangoel by Karen Williams and Khadra Mohammed

Thunder Boy Jr. by Sherman Alexie

The Name Jar by Yangsook Choi

My Name Is Yoon by Helen Recorvits

My Name Is Bilal by Asma Mobin-Uddin

My Name Is Elizabeth! by Annika Dunklee

STEP 2: GRADUALLY RELEASE STUDENTS TO UNCOVER THE CHARACTER'S IDENTITY AND DISPOSITION TOWARD HER NAME

Read the next few lines with the whole group, asking kids to work with a partner to add to their own webs. In the previous lesson, kids were primed with the language that signals identity, and they have an anchor chart from the identity web lesson to support them. (It would be worth adding *name* to the Identity chart if it is not already there.)

STEP 3: MODELING STORYTELLING

After you have read the text aloud and kids have tried it on their own as well, use the kinds of details provided in the story to help you share the story of your name with students. This gives students a model for the work they'll soon be doing. Here's how I introduce mine:

> So, we just heard Esperanza talk about her name and reveal so much of how she feels about her identity. She gives us her thoughts and feelings throughout the piece. Did you guys know my big sister named me? Yep, my mom asked her and my other sister what they wanted their baby sister to be named, and that is what they came up with! My big sister is kind of a boss at home, so that makes sense.
>
> I can use Esperanza's description of her name as a mentor here, to help me figure out what else to tell you about my name. What else does she tell us? She tells us what her name means. Oh, my name means princess in Hebrew and in Arabic. But I also know it is a religious name that is in the Quran, the holy book of Islam, like the Bible or the Torah. You know

how on the first day of school, I told you that my teachers always used to get my name wrong? That's why I wanted you to say your names for me, so I heard the way you say them, rather than just guessing. I was always so embarrassed when teachers would say "Sara(h)" because then I had to stand out to correct the teacher.

After modeling the storytelling, ask them to think about the story of their own name, anything they may know about it, or the feelings they have about their name. Have them think or even write if they need to for a short time. Prompt them to be ready for a turn and talk.

STEP 4: PARTNER INTERVIEWS

Have kids turn and talk with someone near them about their name. Let them know it is OK for now if they don't know much about it. Adults have lived with their names for much longer and have more of a history with their names. This is a good time to talk about sharing the air as well.

I am going to give you guys two minutes to talk about your names. If there are two of you, what does that mean for the time you each get to talk? When we tell stories we get so excited that we go on forever, or we don't always listen to the speaker because we start making connections. So make sure you really listen and honor your partner's name story. Show them it means a lot for them to listen and vice versa.

Because you asked kids to be excellent listeners for their partner, it's now fair game to say to them: "Who had a partner with an interesting story of their name?" I often find myself faking a joke here, like, "Everyone's hand should be up! But do ask your partner quietly if they mind your shar-ing." It helps to break the ice and to remind them of some social skills of a good listener. Asking students to share what they heard reinforces that you are looking for the good listeners, not just the kids who want to share the most. Kids may all want to share, so prepare them by warning that you will take only a set amount—maybe two or three—before moving on.

STEP 5: NOTICING THE CRAFT

Now it's time to back into the text and, with the kids, read like a writer—that is, notice the craft moves and style choices the writer made to convey her feel-ings to the reader or, in this case, the importance or significance of the meaning of her name.

You might make this transition by saying something like this to students:

OK, we just learned about Esperanza's name and also a little bit about our own names. Let's see if we can look at how Sandra Cisneros revealed Esperanza's name to us through her beautiful writing. She left us some strong language but also some clues about her identity in her name.

You might ask these questions:

- *What do you notice about the way Sandra Cisneros wrote this piece?*
- *What do you notice about her sentences, her language, the way they speak to us?*
- *Can you hear the voice of Esperanza? If so, when do you hear it best?* (Read a few lines out loud again with feeling as you consider this with the class.)

During the discussion, make a list of the craft moves that the class identifies. (In the Cisneros story, this list often includes short sentences and metaphors.)

STEP 6: WRITING WITH THE MENTOR IN MIND

Tell the students that they can write their stories using Cisneros' piece as a mentor text.

We can try to write our stories of our names just like Sandra did for Esperanza. She can be a mentor to us in this way.

On a document camera or on chart paper, try it out for your own name in front of them. Go back to the story you told about your name and think aloud as you write. Writing cold in front of kids models the risk-taking and vulnerability we ask them to have each day at school. But if you think it would go better for you to write it ahead of time, just remember that you had a little practice when they embark on their own writing assignment for the first time. In Step 3, I talked to the kids about my name a bit and recollected some personal history, thoughts, and feelings. Remind them that what they just shared in their partner interviews was a form of rehearsing the story and that may help them begin to put pencil to paper.

I am thinking about the story I just shared about my name and I am trying to find the parts that I can match to the mentor text here.

I write, beginning, as Cisneros does, with the meaning of my name: *In Hebrew and in Arabic, it means* princess . . . .

You don't need to write an entire piece—a couple of sentences will likely be enough for them to start thinking of how they will craft their own. Send them off to write in their own spaces. If there are students who are unsure of the origin of their name, they can have time to research their name and consider questions to ask at home. Let students know that these pieces will be shared with the class.

STEP 7: SHARE

Bringing the class back together for a share is a great way to celebrate the writing they have tried. They can also do this in small groups, which may be more comfortable with a personal piece like this. While the writing is important, the bigger lesson here is the empathy being built: names are unique in that they carry value to others in a way we don't have license to label.

Sharing that idea with your class may sound like this:

> *Names that sound different or "weird" to you are normal and important to others and vice versa. The name* ____ **(any name that is extremely common; there may even be multiples in your room)** *may not be a common name in other parts of the world. Alphabets are different; language and meaning are different. Family histories are different. So when you come across a name that sounds "weird" to you, try to see it as unique to that person, their culture, or their family. The best thing you can do if you encounter a new name is to respectfully ask, "Would you say your name for me, please? I want to make sure I get it right."*

↑ FOLLOW-UP

You might display students' name stories in the class, share them in a campfire setting (in a circle on the rug), or hang them on the walls of the classroom for others to interact with. Showcasing student writing at the beginning of the year has the added benefit of helping kids see themselves as writers. Before you present the stories, allow students some time at home to learn more about their name if they don't yet know its full story or meaning. These name pieces also make great gifts for families and even better portfolio pieces to revisit. As students gain insights about their names, you might also encourage them to add what they've learned to their identity webs.

As students encounter more names—in texts or in real life—model using this lens for connections and compassion.

⇅ ADDRESSING TENSIONS

1. Students don't think their name has a good story.

Try this: Researching the origins of their name is always a good place to start. What they find may give them some questions to discuss at home. Looking up other people in history who have the same name is a fun way to research as well. Encourage them to ask someone at home if their name was decided before they were born or on the day of their birth.

2. Students are uncomfortable with their names.

Try this: If you have students who don't want to use their given names and prefer nicknames that blend in with their classroom community, it may help to have multiple read-alouds or texts on hand that can help bring in more globally diverse names. Pull names and photos of well-known athletes (think Olympians) from all around the world. Taking the time to confer with students one-on-one is helpful and supportive when they are uncomfortable.

I would never force a member of my classroom community to use a name that they don't want to use, but I would try to casually talk with that student about the history of the name they've chosen. What is the motivation to use it?

To avoid a situation in which a student has to correct your pronunciation of his or her name during roll call, consider asking students to say their names instead, while you check the name against your roster, making a note of any name preferences or a helpful way to remember pronunciation for next time.

3. Kids don't take names that are *different* seriously.

I once began a read-aloud where the character had a name that was unfamiliar to the students in my class that year. The first page introduced the character and as I began reading, the kids all started snickering or going, "Whaaaaat?" I nearly lost my temper. It took me a moment to recognize that I hadn't taken steps to avoid this issue. I resolved not to miss that opportunity again.

Try this: Frontload the character's name or culture to kids ahead of time. We can model for them something as simple as having them try to pronounce it with you or explore the name through an inquiry lens, asking, "What do you notice?" Normalize the name for them. Research popular names in other countries and in America. Clue them in that in other places in the world, people would find their names incredibly hard to pronounce. We want to get names correct to do right by the person and to help decenter Anglo-Western names as the norm, so as not to deem other names "weird" or even unique.

Journeying into Our Family Histories

"Where I'm From" Poems

What Are "Where I'm From" Poems?

"Where I'm From" poems are, simply, poems that include objects and details about the writer's identity. They use a structure based on George Ella Lyon's poem "Where I'm From," a poem that is, essentially, a list of tangible bits and memories of the writer's identity. Lyon has invited others to write their own "Where I'm From" poems on her website, www.georgeellalyon.com/where.html.

Why Use Identity Poems?

We use poetry for this work because writing poetry helps kids to focus on the specific people, places, things, and ideas that are meaningful to them, not just labels or vague descriptions of who they are. Poetry is accessible and identity has been a long-time theme of poetry. Identity poems can be used as icebreakers but, like identity webs, they are more than that. They are a window into the lives of your students, a stepping-stone toward rapport and mutual respect in your room.

As with any tool for starting to build community, the focus is on how you use the tool, not on the tool itself. If we use poems as a way to learn about the kids—reading the poems, responding to them, conferring with students about the things they wrote, having peer

> I'm from roots as old as an African tree.
> Vietnamese soups and Pakistani spicies.
> (That taste just like home to me.)
>
> I'm from the groovin streets of Manhattan, where everything is alive.
> From the uptown to the downtown.
> Or the unique streets of Karachi.
>
> From the many Z's in my siblings names, and the childish habbits wich I sill carry around.
>
> My responsibilities are as big as my personality.
>
> My family tree lies everywhere even in places I don't know of.

conferences—we are sending the message that kids' backgrounds are valuable not only to them but also to the classroom community. They are a celebration of the diversity of identity in the class as much as they are a way for kids to find similarities with one another.

When Could Identity Poems Be Used?

- When introducing yourself to your students, finding ways to connect to them, and helping them connect to one another.
- When introducing a writing unit early in the year, a biography unit, or content-area inquiry unit.
- When "getting into the character's shoes": if you are asking students to empathize with someone from a culture different from their own, they can use their poems as a point of comparison.
- In summer professional development sessions with your colleagues. They can be hung as a welcome to students so they see their teachers are writers too, and that unpacking and valuing identity at the school matters.

STEP 1: INTRODUCE THE MENTOR POEM

You will need copies of George Ella Lyon's "Where I'm From" in its entirety (available on the poet's website). I usually introduce the poem by projecting the first few lines and reading them aloud.

With identity on their minds, lead kids through a group think-aloud on what this piece could potentially be about. You might begin with something like this:

> We are going to be reading a poem together today from the poet George Ella Lyon. The title is "Where I'm From." Now it might be too obvious that this poem is going to tell us where the poet is from. But that could be done in maybe a word or a sentence. Instead, she dedicated a whole poem to that idea. What other details might she include in a poem about where she is from? Turn and talk.

Give kids about a minute to talk with someone while you lean in to listen. Take three or four answers from partnerships, remembering to celebrate collaborative thinking with prompts such as: "What is something you and your partner came up with?" or with stems such as *"We* thought maybe . . ." or "My partner and I said . . ." That quick language fix honors multiple voices and even promotes a little humility: it helps students to see that they were able to come up with new ideas because they had thinking partners. Win-win!

Other Mentor Texts for Identity Poetry

"Where I'm From" is a powerful poem, but it's just one option for this lesson. Other options include:

Maya Angelou's "Phenomenal Woman"

Selections from the verse novels *Out of the Dust* by Karen Hesse, *Bronx Masquerade* by Nikki Grimes, *A Long Way Down* by Jason Reynolds, or *Solo* by Kwame Alexander

The opening page of *Caminar,* a novel in verse, by Skila Brown (the page is titled "Where I'm From")

Jeannie Baker's beautiful, nearly wordless picture book *Mirror,* which shows how objects give clues to people's identity

Once students understand what an identity poem is, you can also ask them if they know of any other examples of this particular voice in writing.

STEP 2: READ THE MENTOR POEM TOGETHER

Launch into the poem with a quick transition: "OK, let's find out what she has to say about where she is from." Students can follow along (either on their own copies or on the projected version) as you read the poem aloud, stopping to think aloud along the way. The poem includes regional and cultural references that might not be familiar to my students, but I don't stop to think aloud every time I encounter them, as that breaks up the poem. Instead, I may model writing a quick note in the margin while thinking out loud for the first one or two questions—"I wonder what 'He restoreth my soul' means—I'll jot a question mark in the margin here and keep reading"—and then write subsequent questions silently as I keep reading if I need to. Read it a few times to yourself before reading it with the kids, so you can anticipate where you may want to stop to have some group think time.

At the end, let them know you have a question for them to discuss with a partner in a turn-and-talk:

What do we know about George's identity? What identity objects is she revealing about where she is from? Try and use some text evidence from the poem to support your thinking.

If kids are hesitant to start, consider asking them if they'd like to hear the poem again before they talk.

When kids are sharing with a partner, make sure that the screen is visible to them or that they have their own copies to refer to.

After a few minutes, bring the group back together and ask for their thoughts. Take three to five nuggets of collaborative thinking, highlighting the text as they share. If someone shares something that highlights any misconceptions, ask: "Can you show us the text in the poem that helped you come up with that?" Keeping the focus on what the speaker is actually saying in the poem models the expectations you have for the class—rather than making assumptions about someone's identity, listen and be respectful of how each person describes his or her own identity. Help students to go beyond what is most obvious to the eye, like physical attributes. Nudge students to focus more on tradition, experiences, and language—all things that go back to the initial identity anchor chart you made in the first lesson of this book.

STEP 3: USE THE POEM AS A MENTOR TEXT

Now we'll get kids ready to write their own poems:

We have talked about George Ella Lyon's identity based on what we could conclude from her writing. We have used the poem for evidence to help us support our thinking. Now, we'll look at the lines of the poem to help us write one of our own, paying close attention to the types of objects, actions, and language she uses to show us her identity. We can write like George about our own family histories of where we are from using common objects, language, phrases, and memories that come from home or our communities.

There are several examples online of templates people have made using this poem as a model. These templates give the structure of the poem, but leave blanks for people to replace the poet's words and experiences with their own. Students have written the poem both ways in my classes, one having a stronger scaffold than the other.

Here is an example of what that may look like in the first two lines:

Line 1: I am from _____ (common items at your house)

Line 2: From _____ (brands or products you always see when in your home)

Looking through the structure with kids will help them start to brainstorm what they might include in their own poem.

Let's take a look at how she structured her poem. Here, in the first lines, she has named some household items that were always around her house: clothespins and bleach. We have our own common items in our homes, things that are around all the time. Like for me, I always had a lot of rubber bands around the house. I think it is because my sisters and I all had a paper route. (I get funny looks here; I definitely have to explain delivering papers door to door on your bike to some of today's kids!) *Then, a few lines later, she describes her yard—part of her home. If we look at the poem, we can tell the kinds of things that she's naming.*

So every time I read a line from her poem where she mentions a product, object, person, place, or even an event or action, we can think of the same kind of thing in our own lives and replace her examples with ours.

One way to help you is to visualize what you see when you walk in the front door, stand outside, or walk into your bedroom. How would you describe those things to people?

STEP 4: INDEPENDENT WORK TIME TO BRAINSTORM, PLAN, AND DRAFT

Send kids back to their seats to try some planning and writing on their own. You can direct them back to their identity web or name story if they are looking for inspiration. You can also suggest that if they get stuck at a particular spot in the poem, they make a note to talk to an adult at home to consider what their "I Am From" poems might include. I have even paused to do a little visualization with them—eyes closed, trying to see if they can picture their rooms, homes, neighborhoods—and then they just list the things they see. The list becomes the plan from which they can grow their poem.

As they are working and you are roving around the room conferring, you may notice it helps some kids if you offer alternative ways to plan their writing: talking things out or even sketching their rooms, homes, or neighborhoods. If you'd like to share another mentor text with kids in small groups or conferences, you could show them a version of an "I Am From" poem that you've written earlier or another version from a different author—there are many examples online.

Here are a few lines from my own poem I may share with kids as I confer or in the whole group mini-lesson, depending on whether kids need the extra support.

I am from newspaper rubber bands.

From Solo detergent and Bactine.

From glow-in-the-dark prayer beads always facing East.

I am from creamy lasagna and handmade samosas.

These are common household items for me, but right away I reveal a piece of my identity web and items from my home that are unique to my family and our religion. I can use that line as a jumping-off point for a conversation about how my parents have objects around the house that are important to their religion, or about my mom's signature samosas (to make all food OK to talk about).

As you confer, you can nudge students to share their cultural objects, traditions, and family members' names within their poems, pointing back to the mentor texts and highlighting places where the authors have included specific cultural details, not just general terms. By using your own notes or completed poem as a mentor text, you model how you are bringing a piece of your home to the reader.

STEP 5: SHARE

In partners or at tables, have students share what they have so far, with the understanding that these are works in progress. Invite listeners to look for any connections they may have or to ask a question if they are really listening to their partner. We want to encourage genuine sharing and feedback here that sounds the way we modeled it in the lesson:

> *How would you describe those objects? Is there a saying in your home language or a name that you could add here to reveal more of your identity?*
>
> *Tell me more about . . . .*

After sharing, kids may need another minute or two to add some ideas that were ignited from their talks with peers.

Poems will not be completed by the end of a single class. This is just the initial immersion into the writing. How they complete this work is up to you. Will your students take their work home to interview their families and explore their homes and photographs a bit more? Will they have time to draft during the next class period or that evening for homework if they choose?

As a result, the share can be as wide or as narrow as you'd like. How will the histories of your students be shared with the classroom community? With the larger community? I would ask kids what they want to do with these poems as well. Take ideas from them on how to "go public": blogs, having a share of artifacts at school, publishing in school publications, author's chair in the classroom, and gallery walks noticing each other's work are all options to consider.

↑ FOLLOW-UP

The most important parts of this lesson are not the poems but these conversations, which happen as a result of the writing. The self-reflection, the home-school connection, the respect and empathy building are the ultimate goals of this lesson. They may even be schema building: I may choose to bring in or show a picture of the prayer beads I wrote about in my poem so they can then go forward in life having a better understanding of a religion they may not practice but that others do.

Revisit this lens of noticing and studying artifacts in any literature, news, or history you approach for the rest of the year, taking note of how inanimate objects carry great weight for individuals and societies. This always brings the work back to the students; nothing is ever in isolation when doing the work of identity and social comprehension. We are constantly searching for connection.

⇅ ADDRESSING TENSIONS

1. **Students don't think they have anything to put down or write.**

    Try this: As suggested in the lesson, give students who need to draw or sketch what they "see" time to do that during independent work time. That may be a springboard for you to ask them open-ended questions and give them some support on what they can add. It is often hard to notice the everyday things we take for granted around us. Look for any stories hiding in their sketches that would match up with the mentor text used. Use your own poem to show students where you got stuck and to help find any connections you may have to them. Saying something as quick as, "Hey, I noticed in your identity web (or name story) that you talked about basketball a lot; can you say a little more about that so it is clear for me? What types of things do basketball players have lying around the house? What do you hear your parents or other people shouting at a basketball game?"

2. **Students can't get past naming ubiquitous material things.**

    I have had students write things like "I am from the Xbox or the iPhone." These items are so ubiquitous that they may not, at first, give clues about students' unique identities.

    Try this: It is up to us to find out how these items are special to the kids. Do they identify as a gamer? Is this how they spend much of their time?

You can also help students to include more than just these items. Refer back to the mentor poem and notice with students the range of items it includes and the scope of connections the items have to the poet's life: it doesn't include only the things the poet likes best; it includes the things that are so familiar to her—good and bad—that they feel like they are part of her. And these parts of her can tell a story, like the auger. Ask your kid writers: "What items might help to show what is unique about you? What specific stories would these objects tell if they could about you and your history?"

3. **Kids try to make their personal experiences conform.**

I once had a student who mentioned her grandma and grandpa in her poem, but later admitted, "Well, I don't call my grandparents *Grandma* and *Grandpa* like other kids do. I call them something in Russian." Another student said, "I was going to write the Spanish word for the dish my mom always makes, but I wrote it in English instead."

Try this: When kids make edits like these, they are feeling the pressures of conformity, of what is centered in society as *normal*. When modeling writing your own "I Am From" poem, include details that show the language of your own culture, whether it be a vernacular twang, a bit of regional vocabulary, or words from another language (for instance, I often include some of the things my mother lovingly shouts at me at home). Then, should you find that a student is editing out his or her authentic voice, refer back to your own piece, pointing out how it uses the real language of your culture. If kids see you showcasing pieces of culture, and even talking to them about making that special choice to honor it, they will feel empowered to do the same.

4. **Kids seem reluctant to name any items or details.**

When I was a kid, I was always embarrassed by the smells of spices and fried onions from our kitchen at home that clung to my clothes; it was mortifying to have a locker smell like that in a hallway of laundry detergent-smelling kids. I would do anything to avoid bringing attention to it.

Try this: This is where knowing your students really matters. If you are conferring with a student and they seem reluctant to write anything down or to talk through some visualizing, don't press them—their reluctance may be based on embarrassment. Rather than calling them out on this, encourage them to think of another space they identify with and describe that.

Synthesis: Making Thinking Visible

The study of identity is no simple task—it requires both you and your students to navigate the waters of uncertainty, certainty, and wonder. Moreover, as kids grow, they are constantly evolving a new sense of self. Stepping back or beginning the year with a study of *them* will allow them to feel valued and visible in the classroom. These lessons also make their thinking visible.

If you haven't already introduced your class to the "At First I Thought . . . Now I Think" journal structure, do so now. See the introduction for a description of the journal and a reproducible journal page. If they've already begun their work in this journal, ask them to return to it after you've worked through the lessons in this chapter. You might ask them to consider how their thinking has changed about themselves and about others.

2

Listening with Love

It's spring. One of the first times you open your classroom windows after a long, cold winter. Outside, the breeze is sweet and the sun is shining. But here, in my classroom, my eighth-grade class is painfully still, listening as Christina, a girl who is usually bubbly and outgoing, speaks in a strangely quiet voice. Tears are rolling down her face. Our conversation about identity has moved into a discussion of stereotypes, and Christina is recalling some of the labels she's heard applied to herself and to her Mexican-American family: *taco eaters, lazy spics, wetbacks, illegals.*

One of her classmates next to her rubs her shoulder. The room is silent. Another friend grabs a tissue for her. I restrain myself from trying to jump in and save the moment. I want to honor the thinking, listening, and growth that can happen in these gaps of silence and discomfort. My heart is aching for her, but I trust that Christina's classmates will listen and be present for her.

"I am sending Christina a heart," says one student. She forms a heart with index fingers and thumbs and shoots it over to Christina. About a third of the class silently follows suit.

She smiles that closed-mouth smile we all know.

In that moment, there is an immediate sense of family in that classroom. Hands go up, and the conversation continues. The students' honest listening has both supported their classmate and empowered them to take risks and struggle with some very mature ideas that most adults cannot discuss. It's not hard to imagine how this situation might have taken an ugly turn: other students feeling uncomfortable with the weight of Christina's words might have become defensive, might have sneered, might have jumped in to try to explain away her hurt and, in the process, minimized her and her experience. Or worse, imagine how we, as teachers, might have instinctively tried to diffuse discomfort in the classroom with a comment such as, "Oh, my! Well, I'm sure that won't happen to you"—a remark that can be in danger of erasing Christina's truths and fears. But this class knew that what was really needed here was listening, learning, and empathy. Kid to kid; no need for me to step in and save the struggle. They had her back.

If we want our kids to truly respect one another we have to meet them where they are, consider interactions from their perspectives, and find teachable moments along the way.

Not all of my students learned to listen the way Christina's class did. Earlier in my career, long before Christina was my student, I was ambitious to have my class agreement (or class constitution, compact, or contract) done on day one of school. I can still remember the point in the lesson where each year's new students would sit on the rug with me and listen as I *told* them what should be on the chart and then invited them to add a few ideas. Each year, the students would dutifully acquiesce, recalling rules from every previous school year: *Raise your hand to speak. Respect each other. One person speaks at a time.* And on and on. Their Class Contract game was on point! On autopilot, even.

And, during the year, any time I needed to, I could direct students' attention to that chart—the one we had made "together." I was doing a ton of superficial reminding, and they were doing a ton of compliant parroting. Looking back, I wonder: What did those kids learn from that experience? What message did I send if this is how we set up class "agreements"? I fear it was that listening means silence. That respect equals compliance.

I meant well with this work. I wanted to give my students tools that would help us listen to one another and build a respectful community. Spelling out a list for them seemed like the most direct way to do it. But, as Peter Johnston (2012, 69) reminds us, "The problem with apprenticing children into humanity—the intellectual and social life of society—is that much of the action we want them to understand takes place inside people's heads." If we want our kids to truly respect one another, if we want them to listen to each other and actually hear what they are saying, we have to meet them where they are, consider interactions from their perspectives, and find teachable moments along the way. What does "respect" look like, sound like, feel like? We cannot use one-size-fits-all anchor charts; no two classes I've ever had would operate authentically under the same norms. (Do *any* two communities we know follow the exact same norms?)

If we want kids to attend to the multiple perspectives around them and listen actively and empathetically, we need to mentor them and show them how. I purposely use *mentor*, and not *teach*, because we need to be practicing these skills ourselves rather than just telling them to do so.

In this chapter, I can only sketch a blueprint and offer some tried-and-true suggestions and teaching moves. You, the expert in your classroom, will need to choose the moments and tools you'll use to help your students build the skill of active listening.

The most important guidance I can give you here is to provide safe opportunities to do the social comprehension work of listening every day. Our goal is to make the process of active listening automatic in their thinking and writing, and to treat listening to someone else as an act of love. To do this, we need to give kids plenty of opportunities to make this type of thinking visible in our dialogical classrooms. These opportunities need to be real enough that kids will use the skills they learn in our classrooms in their lives beyond school. That may mean catching "live" moments in the classroom or in the halls and using them as teachable moments, rather than setting up plausible, yet inauthentic scenarios.

There are few absolutes in social comprehension; full immersion in it often yields more questions than answers. This work is messy because it is authentic and because it deals with human beings. So, I humbly ask (maybe even humbly implore) you to head into this work with a commitment to uncertainty, while understanding the value of how it can better our citizenship in this big world:

Active, empathetic listening facilitates real communication. How many times have you so misread or misinterpreted what someone was thinking or saying that you jumped to an emotional reaction? (I am personally raising many fingers here.) Out of those times, would pausing to practice an active listening stance have helped to avoid that impulse? (Now, I am liberally nodding.) Paulo Freire (2000) explains that "[s]olidarity requires true communication . . . only through communication can human life hold meaning." Creating opportunities where we practice the critical components of communication—how to listen, pause, speak, ask questions, and reflect—can yield the solidarity we need.

Active, empathetic listening facilitates real learning. Listening requires us to consider and utilize perspective, evidence, and language, connecting the new to the known, and we evolve as a result. Kids become the teachers in dialogical classrooms where real communication and real learning take place.

Let's get started.

Introduce Active Listening by Giving Kids a Chance to Show What They Already Know

Before students can become skilled, active listeners, they need to understand what active listening looks like, sounds like, and feels like. The following activity gives students an opportunity to show what they already know about active listening.

1. Tell students that, in a few minutes, you'll ask them to discuss something in pairs or small groups, with the goal of "actively listening" to their partner(s).

2. Read or view a piece of text or media with students that will elicit a conversation—preferably one that has enough depth for them to discuss, agree and/or disagree, and draw on their background knowledge. I like Shirley Jackson's "The Lottery," Toni Cade Bambara's "Raymond's Run," Gary Soto's "Seventh Grade," and Jacqueline Woodson's *The Other Side*.

3. Before sending the students into their pairs or groups, ask a student volunteer to model this conversation with you while the rest of the class watches. Ask the class to look for and note signs that you and the student are listening actively.

4. As you converse with the student, use the signals of active listening—cues that show interest and genuine listening:

   • **Body position:** Knee to knee, eye to eye, shoulders square to each other, best eye contact possible. "Give them your best shoulders and your best eye contact," I say.

   • **Making notes:** Taking mental notes, writing notes, or recording what others say.

- **Follow-up questions** such as:

  ✳ Can you say more about that? I need more information to make sure I am understanding you.

  ✳ I heard you say _____; can you give me an example of what you mean?

  ✳ Did I hear you correctly when you said _____?

  ✳ I'm curious. What makes you say that?

  ✳ Can you talk a little bit about how you came to that conclusion?

5. After your fishbowl demonstration, ask the students how you and your partner indicated that you were listening actively. Scribe their responses on an anchor chart. In my classes, I've often titled these charts "Our Zone" or a variation on that name, such as "Our Discussion Zone," "Our Reading Zone," or "Our Listening Zone." Whatever title you use for the chart, be sure it underscores that these signs of active listening belong to the class as a whole. As you add ideas to the chart, include the students' initials next to their contributions. For example:

   - Take some silent time to *listen* to how your body is feeling. (LC)

   - *Hear* each other, then empower each other to take risks. (MC)

   - *Notice* . . . and send hearts to your friends when they need them. (AS)

6. Let students begin their own pair or small-group discussions. As they work, circulate in the room and look for ways in which they are showing active listening.

7. Bring the class back together and invite them to share in a way that puts listening first:

   When we hear from you, I want you to focus on what you took away from listening to your partner(s). That means, rather than saying what is on your mind or making your contribution to the group, you are instead going to amplify or echo what your partner(s) offered.

8. Work with students to add to your zone chart examples of active listening that they saw in others.

Build Listening Skills Across the Year

"Our Zone" anchor charts are working documents. When we observe someone doing something we could all emulate to become better at active listening, I jot it on a sticky note and attach it to the chart. If we find that we can actually activate that move and that it helps us, we write it directly on the chart for permanent use.

When heated talks arise, when we need to listen better, when we talk over each other, when we need to manage the way we disagree—these are the best times to build these charts. Often, I direct students back to our charts when I set up a lesson in which I know we will need to use active listening:

Today, we are going to discuss a topic that may get heated. What do we need to do in our zone to allow for strong opinions but maintain who we are during our discussion?

Then we revisit the chart. But lots of times something arises in the middle of a lesson that I can't anticipate, like Christina's brave moment, and we need to regroup, consider the ideas on our chart, and strategize next steps.

You may find yourself moving out of the listening zone because you are getting frustrated or upset, and that is fine. The important thing is that you notice and name it first. Take a minute to find a strategy that will work for you to get back into the zone or take a quick break.

Tools and Ideas for Modeling, Spotting, and Naming

As I mentioned in the opening pages of this chapter, presenting kids with a list of rules is not as effective as we might hope in promoting active listening. However, it may be helpful for you, as the teacher, to have a range of tools at your fingertips to help you identify and name what kids are doing well. This is where kid watching during class and during the least-structured times of their day (between classes, recess, lunch) helps. You can catch kids or adults listening actively in the wild and then name what you saw as something to try out.

This list can also remind you of what you might model in class on a daily basis. I share the following lists in the hope that you'll use whatever suggestions are helpful in a particular situation, exploring a single idea or two with students when the time is ripe, and considering if/how to add them to your own zone charts.

Actions and Words for Acknowledging the Thoughts of Others

- *Smiling. High-fiving. Fist bumps. Shaka signs.*
- "Something that [partner's name] said that stayed with me was. . . ."
- "I never even thought of _____ until [partner's name] mentioned it."
- "I wanted to acknowledge something that [partner's name] said. . . ."
- "_____ helped me think about. . . ."

Actions and Words for Agreeing

- *Smiling. High-fiving. Fist bumps. Shaka signs.*
- "[Partner's name] and I both. . . ."
- "We both talked/thought/agreed/discussed/decided/used. . . ."
- "We have similar thoughts or evidence about. . . ."

Actions and Words for Disagreeing Respectfully

- *Smiling. Handshakes. Fist bumps. Shaka signs.*
- "My partner and I actually disagree on this idea." (Then teach them both how to say what they are each thinking unless they have agreed to have one spokesperson.)
- If there is a spokesperson: "We actually didn't see eye to eye. One of us thinks _____, and the other thinks _____."
- "I heard what others had to say, which was _____ [have them name it so it is not misrepresented] and I still felt like _____ because _____."

- "We need to take some time to think more. We are agreeing to disagree for now."

- "I am having a hard time understanding. . . ."

- "I respect your experiences and opinion, and/but. . . ." *(Note the fine nuance between* and *and* but.)

- "Can you say more about that? I want to make sure I understand where you are coming from."

- "I hear you. . . ."

- "Can I tell you what I hear you saying?"

- "Can you try to see where I am coming from before you respond?"

- "Thanks for making an effort to understand where I'm coming from/what I am trying to say."

- "I appreciate that we can talk about this even though we are coming from two different places."

- "I don't have an informed opinion on that."

- "I know that I disagree with what you are saying, but I also need time to build a more informed opinion to discuss this."

Tools for Managing Discomfort During Disagreement

The work of social comprehension, while powerful, is not always comfortable. Social comprehension strives for awareness and understanding, not consensus or compliance. So there may be points on which people will never agree. Rather than letting discomfort lead us to defensiveness or a need to argue our position over someone else's, we can acknowledge the awkwardness and look for ways to move ahead productively.

- Enter the conversation with the intent to learn something.

- Commit to the possibility of being uncomfortable at some point.

- Notice the feeling of that discomfort: How is your body responding?

- Expect that someone will disagree with any opinion you have.

- Understand the value in listening to someone else's perspective.

- Before you speak your truth, consider: Are there ways others may see this?

Our Zone
Agreements for Real Conversations

- We consider our own identity & the identity of others → & the identity of our community!
- We create a safe space to take risks & be brave! (We enter with a Learning stance)
- We are the owners of our conversations (our comments, questions, ideas)
- We problem solve CREATIVELY & TOGETHER
- We are observers of the world around us

Co-Created Charts to Support Active Listening

As you and your students name strategies and tools that help you to listen actively, use anchor charts to make sure these ideas are available when kids need them. To give you an idea of what these charts might look like, here are a few that my students and I developed over the school year. While these charts are packed with ideas, they didn't start out that way. Sometimes I would jot down a really great sound bite from a student while they were talking—that one nugget might be the first entry. The charts grew as we gradually added ideas together across the year.

The Art of Disagreeing

- Disagreements are OK!
→ We grow from convos like this ←
- My Partner & I disagreed
Agree→ Both speak their truths
Both listen for perspective

"I don't think we see eye to eye on this."
"Thanks for hearing me out."
"I hear you—and I still feel..." (because)
"I respect your opinion. I just need time to think about it. & maybe figure out why we don't agree."
"Say more about that..."
"Can I tell you what I hear you saying? And please let me know if I'm misunderstanding you."

The Art of Discourse

Discourse is when we talk, think, agree, reflect, disagree, and question → Together
We are engaging in reasoning & understanding

- I hear you...
- I respect your experiences → my experience is...
- This is how I am understanding or seeing it...
- Can you say more about that?
- May I tell you what I hear you saying?
- May I finish first, please?
- I appreciate you sharing that...
- I appreciate being able to talk with you about this..."

Choices you have in Discourse

- Enter the conversation with an intent to learn something from someone else.
- Commit to the possibility of being uncomfortable at some point
- Notice the feeling of that discomfort. How is your body responding?
- Understand people will disagree with an opinion or an idea (of yours)
- Before you speak your truth, consider the ways it may be understood or interpreted
- LISTEN & use language to disarm ↳ART of DISCOURSE

↑↓ ADDRESSING TENSIONS

1. **A discussion erupts into a disagreement where kids could feel attacked.**

   Try this: Having a plan in place before this kind of situation arises is key. You can help your kids to be self-aware of their triggers and to identify strategies for exit points in a conversation. I can guarantee if you start a conversation where you ask, "Have you ever had a moment in a conversation where you were growing increasingly angrier, sadder, or more frustrated by the second, almost to the point of explosion?" you will have hands go up with profuse nodding. Then ask them what it feels like inside as that is happening, just before the point of explosion, and ask volunteers to share a strategy they have used to either calm down or exit the situation. Write those down (perhaps on another "Our Zone" anchor chart) and then have individual kids choose what they think would work for them and why. For example, my kids used to say, *I need a brain break, Ms. Ahmed*, and I knew that meant they needed to chill and would go get a drink and come back. Hold students accountable for applying their chosen strategies as needed.

2. **Students feel compelled to "win" a discussion or disagreement.**

   We want to normalize the idea that there can be disagreement and agreement in any conversation. Remove the assumption that there are winners and losers in difficult discussions. We can mentor kids to value having conversations for the rest of their lives with people who have different ideas and opinions as a result of their experiences and identity.

   Try this: Be a 360-degree observer of your class: look for body language and listen for sounds kids make as well as their words.

   Work with students on eye contact in both positive and challenging situations. Model the language of disagreeing with someone while giving them the respect of eye contact. Ask kids for language they think works better. Don't jump in to try to smooth over moments of disagreement.

   Catch kids using productive language in a difficult conversation and share it with others.

Synthesis: Making Thinking Visible

Make the "At First I Thought . . . Now I Think" chart available to your students periodically, giving students additional pages as necessary, so that they read what they've written in the past, reflect on the heart work they have been doing, and consider their collaborations with classmates.

Encourage them to use language from charts you have created along the way, especially if it is a takeaway that honors another classmate—this shows they have practiced being a better listener. I might even say something like:

> High five to you if, in your reflection, you can give a shout-out to a person
> in this class from whom you learned something specific today or this week.
> Even cooler would be your walking up to that person and telling them how
> they have helped you to learn and grow.

3

Being Candid

There's a slide on the screen that reads *Microaggressions*. I ask a room of adults if they have *heard* the word before. My wording is intentional: I don't want to know who thinks they know the definition; I want to activate some schema of where they may have seen or heard the term. I also want everyone to have some think time.

"Has anyone heard or seen this term before?" Some reluctant hands go up, silently imploring me not to call on them. Interestingly, I see the same pattern when I ask the same question of kids. "Go ahead and turn to someone near you and talk about where you've seen it, heard it, or what it means in your experience."

I do this same strategy with students when introducing a new word or concept. I could just *tell* them a googled definition of *microaggressions* to memorize and keep the lesson moving. Or I could draw from their experiences of having heard or seen the word, activating background knowledge and using each other to *question* and *think* about a new concept, and thus grow a common and more sustainable understanding. The work of social comprehension is truly an inquiry approach.

I bring the adult learners back and invite them to speak into the silence. They begin to call out:

"When an AV guy takes my laptop from me, assuming I can't do it myself."

"What mix are you?"

"Can I touch your hair?"

"Tell me about your culture."

"Speaking *louder* to me because they assume I don't speak English."

I join in and add one: "People always asking me where I am from, and I answer, 'Chicago.' They respond, 'No, where are you really from?'"

41

All of the shared responses betray a hurt or an anger or a smarting sense of injustice. But they are honest and they are harbored by the individual for a reason. So many people carry these small moments of great impact with them for a lifetime. Talking about them is the first step in stopping them. By sharing our stories of microaggressions, we can help others to see and avoid them. By listening to others' stories of microaggressions, we can learn to see instances when we've impressed microaggressions on others, even inadvertently.

Chapter 1 ended with kids feeling visible in the classroom community. Their own webs, their given names, their stories of family history hiding in material objects and experiences at home all build toward a healthy and confident sense of self. In Chapter 2, we looked at the skill of active listening. In this chapter, we'll explore identity even further, beyond the pieces that are shared lightly. We'll move into the territory of honest—and sometimes hard—truths, assumptions, and perspectives. We will focus on being *candid*, a little more honest with ourselves, with the intent to evolve. Candor requires a self-awareness and sincerity that isn't always easy and doesn't always feel good in the moment, but it has the power to constructively move us forward, together.

Candor requires a self-awareness and sincerity that isn't always easy and doesn't always feel good in the moment

Now that you've worked with your kids to help them gain some familiarity with self, you'll use the things they know and can proudly claim about their identity to gauge how all those identifiers affect the way they relate to the people and conversations around them. In this chapter, you'll be side-by-side with students to address bias and engage in some accountable talk—both self-talk and group talk. The goal is healthy, candid self-exploration while listening, learning, and being empathetic.

The work in this chapter touches on issues that may be emotionally charged. In my experiences with teachers and students, I've found that the following suggestions have been helpful:

Share personal stories. Sharing personal stories extends an olive branch of self-disclosure. As my parents grow wiser with their years, my father often tells us stories of his youth, and it feels like I know him more than I ever have. Who are those people in your life? Storytelling is a powerful model of candor we can use to gain miles of rapport. I once saw a teacher put her identity web on the doc camera in March—well into the school year. Her students— kids she had worked with for months—were overjoyed to be trusted with these details and glad to find connection points to her. "You speak three languages?! No way! So does my mom!" one student called out. Another exclaimed, "You love dogs and cats as much as me, Ms. Emma!" Shared animal love + mom-level connections = early social comprehension win. Knowing our commonalities helps us when we have difficult conversations.

Pause and be present. Sometimes we are moving so fast that we are always thinking about the next thing to say or do, not taking time to pause and realize the impact of silence. Let kids think. Give them time to muddle around in their feelings. Listen closer. Look out into the sea of faces and do a little kid watching. When it comes to difficult conversations, there is tremendous power in pausing. There are no timed, fill-in-the-bubble correct answers. This is a process.

Honor each student's identity. We'll continue to use our ever-evolving identity webs as a baseline in recognizing the ways our experiences shape our bias, how our messages impact others, and ultimately how our perspectives are formed. To achieve a level of social comprehension that works at school, at home, in teams—virtually any realm where others are present and we interact with them—we must work hard to have a healthy understanding of self and of the implications of our identity in our shared world.

Unpack terms in context. The lessons that follow discuss *perspective*, *bias*, and *microaggressions* (other terms may spring up as well). Unpacking these or other unfamiliar terms with an inquiry stance will help to ensure that students are all working from the same understanding. This will give you a little more traction while diving into the complexities of bias. How you unpack the language and terminology is your call: you might use media clips, quotes from literature, a read-aloud, or a shared text. Once kids have some experience with a particular term, you might work with them to name the feelings, thoughts, and experiences they associate with the term to form a class understanding that is more conceptual than rote. Treating your work together more like an inquiry than a decontextualized vocabulary lesson will make it more personally meaningful and useful in the long run.

Try this work yourself first. As with all of the lessons in this book, I strongly suggest that you dive into the lessons in this chapter before using them with your students. Teaming with a small group of colleagues or as part of a school-wide commitment to personal and professional development in social comprehension (my strongest recommendation) will give you insights that will help you teach these lessons with students. You can tell kids that you're exploring concepts alongside them, but you'll have done some extensive background reading first. Unpredictable things come up in this process and having tried the work yourself is the best way to prepare for how kids *may* respond; this also allows you to talk with them on how it felt for you—candor!

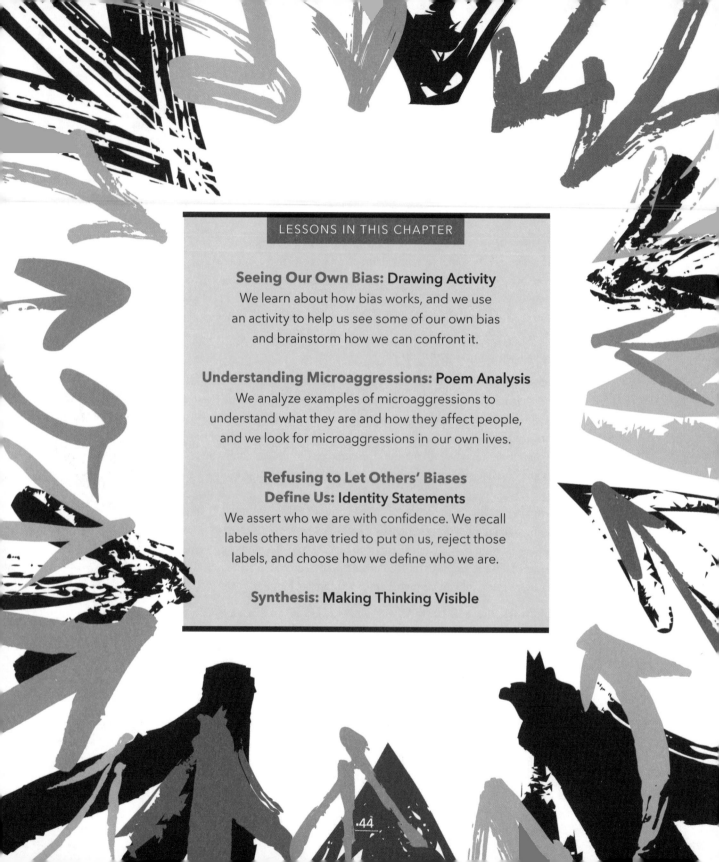

LESSONS IN THIS CHAPTER

Seeing Our Own Bias: Drawing Activity
We learn about how bias works, and we use
an activity to help us see some of our own bias
and brainstorm how we can confront it.

Understanding Microaggressions: Poem Analysis
We analyze examples of microaggressions to
understand what they are and how they affect people,
and we look for microaggressions in our own lives.

**Refusing to Let Others' Biases
Define Us: Identity Statements**
We assert who we are with confidence. We recall
labels others have tried to put on us, reject those
labels, and choose how we define who we are.

Synthesis: Making Thinking Visible

Seeing Our Own Bias

Drawing Activity

What Is Implicit Bias?

Bias is when we have our mind made up about something based on a prior experience, our environment, or some part of our identity. We might admit to being biased regarding things we are comfortable saying, such as, "I may be biased, but aren't my nieces and nephews pretty cute?" I love my nieces and nephews, they're adorable, and I'm happy to be a smitten aunt. But bias is more than showing favoritism toward people you love. It is an unconscious stance—a snap judgment—that is based on all the parts of your identity experience. In the *New York Times* POV video series, Saleem Reshamwala describes implicit bias as "thought processes that happen without you even knowing it; little mental shortcuts that hold judgments you might not agree with."

Biases aren't just something we believe—they're something we act on, operating from many parts of our brain. They are our associations with objects and symbols. How much we trust someone based on looking at them. How much value we place on information given the source. How we tend to feel more comfortable with and compassionate toward those who look like us. Decisions we make every day in our classrooms.

How we view and measure people's character can be quick judgments grounded in our implicit bias.

Why Introduce Bias?

It's important to talk about bias because we can't work against something that we don't know exists. Rarely do we admit, "I may be biased, but I only go to the grocery store where the people look just like me," yet we make choices along these lines every day, consciously and subconsciously. We all have bias. Introducing it to students is a way of making the implicit explicit so they can start to think about their thinking as they consider topics that are social or political—race, guns, human rights, government funding, who

I chose to draw a doctor

they choose as friends, what they choose to read. The sooner we can talk with students about bias, the sooner they can be self-aware. This isn't just an academic exercise: if you've ever felt the sting of a comment or action that was tinged with an unconscious bias, or if you've ever realized with horror that something you've said without malice has been received as racist or sexist or classist, you know how important this work is. It is often the hidden, unintentional forms of bias that are really damaging to marginalized individuals. Discussing bias with kids leads to opportunities to make the implicit explicit. It gives them (and us) the space to learn how those little mental shortcuts our minds make every day can have a greater impact than we realize on our thoughts, on our actions, and on others.

When Could We Discuss Bias?

When is it appropriate to discuss bias? The short answer is, all the time. Understanding bias plays a huge role in students' lives each day and in every lesson in this book. You can also consider examples of bias in your daily teaching routine:

- **In your classroom library.** Do an audit of your own classroom library (and personal library!). Whose voices are heard? Who's telling the stories of history? Are there voices in the library, through authors and characters, that reflect voices in the classroom?

- **In the texts you use for instruction.** Look for a range of perspectives and voices in the sources you use to teach. For example, I have used Howard Zinn's *A People's History of the United States* alongside a general history textbook entry on the same topic to uncover perspective, point of view, and bias.

It is also worth mentioning that there are plenty of implicit bias "tests" and "surveys" out there, such as the Implicit Association Test run by Harvard's Project Implicit. While these tests and surveys can help brave, committed adults to take a hard look at their own biases, I don't recommend giving them to kids. Tools that attempt to measure implicit bias return statistical results and labels, not guidance for growth and change. Starting the work of social comprehension by focusing on students' deficiencies is as likely to result in shock and defensiveness—neither of which is helpful in this work—as it is to lead to openness, vulnerability, and willingness to change. This is not a worksheet curriculum; learning about bias needs to be thoughtfully planned and supported.

STEP 1: INTRODUCE THIS WORK THROUGH A STIMULUS

Invite students to try something without any warm-up:

> *In your journals, I want you to quickly draw or sketch and label one of the following: a doctor, scientist, teacher, athlete, pilot. I am not concerned*

with your artistic ability. We are going to come back to it in a few minutes. You have three minutes to do this. Go!

When the three minutes are up, ask students to label what they drew with one word (e.g., *doctor*), then close their journals and set them aside. Let students know that you'll be returning to their drawings soon.

If you are reading through this lesson for the first time, stop reading here and make the same drawing you'll be asking the kids to do. Give yourself three minutes to sketch, set your drawing aside, and then continue reading.

STEP 2: INTRODUCE THE CONCEPT OF BIAS

As a stimulus to introduce the concept of bias to my students, I often project a picture of the human brain. It helps to make a big concept a little more concrete. Here's how I've done this with my classes:

I am showing you a picture of the brain today because I want to explain to you that it holds something you use every day without even knowing. It's called your bias. *We all have it! Can I see a signal if you have heard or seen the word before?*

If enough kids raise their hands, I have them turn and talk to each other to discuss where they have seen or heard it or to talk about what they think it means.

For example, a group of fifth graders sharing their background knowledge on bias produced this list—a pretty strong start!

- labeling
- assumptions
- favoring
- judging
- real/fake news
- giving an advantage to someone

I write down the list so we can all see it. Then, I talk about and list where bias can come from.

Great list! Thanks for activating your schema on that. So bias grows throughout our lives based on:

- *where we were raised*
- *how and by whom we were raised*
- *our interactions with our friends, peers, and coworkers*
- *our school, community, or religion*

- *the media or news we watch and listen to*

- *the politics we read or hear other people talk about*

- *lots of the things that make up our identity*

Next, I explain some theories about how the brain works, to show why bias can have such a strong effect on our thinking.

Our brain works in two big systems with lots of working parts in each, and both systems help us make sense of our world.

System 1 is the part of the brain that is automatic. It is always instantly reacting, and our brain doesn't even have to be consciously aware. Like if I say, "What is 2 + 2?" **(Inevitably, someone shouts it out and you can say, "That was system 1!")** *We don't turn it on or off; it just runs. This same system is also the part of the brain where we make snap judgments or assumptions. When we look at a person, we sometimes make up a quick story about them before we even get to know them: they are scary, they don't speak English, they are poor, they are cool, they are smart, they are slow and lazy. It happens automatically, without thinking: the messages that go through our mind take a shortcut to our reactions, responses, judgments, labels, emotions, beliefs . . . or our bias. Remember this is all based on where bias comes from.*

System 2 is the system that we use to focus on more logical thinking and concentration—the kind of thinking we do at school, on a long test, while reading directions to assemble something, or while we read and listen to new information to try to make sense of it. It is more controlled and conscious than a snap reaction. We slow down. It takes its time and makes an effort to make sense of something. Remember that person we saw and made up a story about? When we use system 2, we don't assume that a person is scary, poor, or slow: we slow down, understand we don't know them at all, think critically about why we are responding the way we are, and maybe get to know them better.

The important thing is that system 1 is operating completely involuntarily all the time. You just react to things and can't always control your thoughts or feelings. System 2 is in charge of self-control, where we slow down and think something through. We have to call on it to allow for some reasoning.

STEP 3: SHARE AND CONSIDER OUR OWN BIAS

Now ask students to get out their drawings and to consider what they drew.

Go back to your drawings for me. Instead of sharing your drawings, take a moment to consider, with your inner voice, what you decided about how each of these people should look. What gender did you choose? What skin tone? What age? Do these people look like you or unlike you?

To get them comfortable, I ask,

Show us with your hands up . . . how many of you drew a

> *Scientist?*

> *Doctor?*

> *Athlete?*

> *Pilot?*

> *Teacher?*

> *OK, let's do that again, but this time listen to my follow-up.*

> *Hands up if you drew a scientist. Keep your hands up if that scientist is, according to your drawing, a male. Now, how many of you drew a female scientist?*

Do that for the doctor, athlete, pilot, and teacher as well. Kids will start to notice and smile, maybe even be a bit awkward or embarrassed once it clicks what is happening (see the "Addressing Tensions" section). I have noticed some red cheeks here and I always say something like, "You guys are being super honest with yourselves in public right now, and I think that is awesome, because it isn't easy."

Sometimes I add with a smile, "What do you think is going on here? Turn and talk." I do this so they can name their action and hopefully this leads them to become increasingly aware of their bias, rather than my pointing the finger at them for their bias, which we all have. Then, I address the elephant in the room:

Believe it or not, researchers have been asking children to draw a picture of a scientist for decades, just as I asked you to do. Do you know what they've found? Most of the time, kids draw scientists as men, not women (Finson 2002). Some researchers have seen more balance today than a few decades ago, but kids still draw more men than women when they're asked to draw a scientist (Jones and Bangert 2006).

Now, take a moment to think to yourself: What patterns do you see about the choices you made in these drawings? How might those choices show a bias? Perhaps you unconsciously drew a male scientist or pilot because your experiences and all the messages that society sends you suggest that most scientists and pilots are male, and you may not think of women when you think of scientists or pilots. This just means we need to read about more women scientists in this class; there are many!

Turn and talk to someone near you about your drawing if you are comfortable.

Then ask a few partnerships to share—again, if they are comfortable doing so.

Does anyone want to be super courageous and share more about what they drew and their thinking behind it?

Take a few comments from the group. I recently asked a fifth grader to say more about why he drew a male scientist and he quickly responded, "Well, because most scientists are men." The girls all shot him a look and one of them blurted out, "Hello! Marie Curie!" Then we asked him if he'd ever seen the movie *Hidden Figures* or read the book *Ada Twist, Scientist*. The stories we read and movies we watch play a huge part in shaping our bias. He went a little pink in the cheeks and looked at me pleadingly.

Moments like this are crucial in our teaching. In a split second, we have an important choice to make. We could try to "save" the moment, perhaps by saying, "Oh, it's OK! I know you didn't mean anything bad!" and moving on. When we do this, we are trying to rescue kids from discomfort. But if we don't pause to allow kids to understand their own responsibilities in social comprehension, are we really helping them? Instead, we could use this moment, even though it is uncomfortable, to help kids see and feel how this work applies to them. In doing so, we can affirm their effort and remind them that they are in a safe place.

In this situation, I said, "Oh, you know that feeling you have right now? It is you being so aware of your bias. You just activated system 2 and that is awesome!"

Here make sure to address the kids who may have gone against the stereotypical thinking and drawn a female scientist or doctor. Ask them if they are willing to share their thought process (if they can remember it). Ask: Why do you think you drew a female doctor?

Figure 3.1a-b Proud drew a female doctor, she said, because her doctor is female. Yumi drew a female scientist. When I asked what was her thinking behind it, she quickly said, "Oh, I want to be one when I grow up, so I drew myself as a scientist." Another student piggybacked off of Yumi to say that the characters from the movie *Hidden Figures* were female scientists, so that is why she drew one. Stories matter when it comes to bias.

Finding one of our own biases can make us uncomfortable. If you did find a bias just now, know that you're not alone. We all have biases. The important thing is to be honest with ourselves and work through them, not to pretend that we don't have them.

This is not a moment to make kids feel bad about themselves. Most times when I do this, the kids nod with me as I name what gender I think they may have drawn for scientist. If you see evidence of bias in the drawings you made, you can even tell them what you drew, if you're comfortable doing that. This work isn't about shaming people; it's about making the implicit explicit. Honesty is the number one step in creating an antibias classroom environment, and it begins with us.

Ask students:

Does anyone have any questions about bias or the brain?

If they ask questions you don't feel prepared to answer in the moment, list them as a chart and follow up with a mini-inquiry after this lesson so kids can research or discuss further.

STEP 4: ACTIVATE OUR CANDOR

Now I'm going to ask you to be really honest. I want this to be private for now, so you can put your heads down or close your eyes. Knowing what you know about how your brain makes these shortcuts and says or does things that aren't always a good representation of who you think you are, give me a signal if you have ever said or done something that was a reaction or judgment that you wanted to take back. Maybe you hurt someone or got in trouble for something you didn't mean.

Take a quick scan. The scan is not for you to judge the kids who have their hands up (inevitably most of them will, in my experience); it is more to set you up for a quick writing moment coming up.

> *Thanks for your honesty in front of me, but mostly for being candid with yourself. Take a minute just to write about the time you were thinking of. No one will read this and you won't need to share. So just take a minute to be with your thoughts.*

Give students two minutes to write.

> *As we continue to work through our bias and learn about how it can impact the way we make people feel, you may have moments where your mind takes that shortcut and you say or do something that is really hurtful to someone else. And you find yourself saying a lot, "I didn't mean it like that!" Or, "I was just playing around!" Or you may think something that doesn't feel right about a person or a group of people, and you aren't sure why. There are some ways to get through that.*

I scribe on a chart as I talk through these solutions.

> 1. *Acknowledge feelings: Was it your bias talking? What are the feelings of the receiver of the message? How do you feel being accused or on the defense?*
>
> 2. *Think about how the receiver of that message felt having heard it. They can't unhear it. It won't just go away. And maybe their reaction is because you weren't the first person to say it to them either.*
>
> 3. *Think about what to do next and maybe ask. What will work to move forward in a positive way, after saying "sorry"? Is admitting that you misspoke and were wrong a way to move forward?*

> *Maybe in your reflecting or writing you tried these things or saw a moment when you could have used them. It takes practice, and we will work on it.*

> *You can always come to me or talk to an adult you trust about that feeling. If you spot bias in something we read or watch or something you see happening, or if you feel like you are the target of someone's bias-filled action or comments, then bring it up with me, even if you are unsure about it.*

Turn and tell someone one thing that you learned today about your own brain, about bias, or about how not all scientists are men. (I add this last bit with a smile.)

This is a very good place to listen in and to check in with some kids who need support. If you hear anything that is way off your own objective, you can redirect kids individually or as a group. Finish by acknowledging the kids' efforts.

Thanks for your heart work today. I even heard some of you sharing your stories you wrote. So brave and honest.

↑ FOLLOW-UP

Now that kids know the term *bias*, you can help them to see instances of bias in their own experiences and in the texts you study together. This work is ongoing. The steps outlined in the share and the anchor charts you make throughout this lesson are worth having visible in the classroom. You and the kids can reference these steps just as you use literacy and math anchor charts when necessary.

An important thing to remember is that we are not shaming anyone for their bias. This should not be a "gotcha" exercise or a guilt-inducing topic, but rather something to be identified and addressed. That kids are even thinking about it should be noted as a positive. You might say, "I just watched you slow down and activate system 2 because you caught your bias. Awesome!"

Further discussions of bias will also give you opportunities to introduce other language associated with bias: *discrimination, racism, prejudice, sexism,* and *ableism.* These terms are often misconstrued or oversimplified in textbook-ish definitions, but introducing them while considering the bias in a particular situation will help students to understand their full meanings.

↕ ADDRESSING TENSIONS

1. **Kids end up labeling everything as bias. They become the bias police.**

   Try this: Identifying bias is an important observation to make, as we do want kids to think critically about what they read, hear, and see. To ensure that kids' efforts are productive and supportive, I often do the "Home Court" lesson from Nancy Steineke and Smokey Daniels' book, *Mini-Lessons for Literature*

Circles (2004). The lesson invites the kids to consider why teams statistically do better in home games than in away games. The kids usually note that players feel more supported on their home court, and that they can relax because they are surrounded by people who are cheering for them. Then, we discuss how the same rules apply to our classroom environment: when we treat each other with respect, we establish a "home court" where we can all do our best. "Home court" becomes a two-word reminder to respect each other if we hear a put-down, even a joking one. It's a lesson on friendliness and support in the spaces where we feel safest to succeed. (Without fail, a few kids will go around for the rest of the day or the next two days overusing the term *home court* for everything they see. I could take this as mocking the lesson, but I choose to believe that it's great they are still talking about the lesson in context!) A reminder of "home court" can help kids who seem particularly vigilant about pointing out others' shortcomings to reconsider their approach.

You might also confer with students who seem to be arbitrarily labeling everything as bias. Perhaps they are misunderstanding the concept of bias. However, it is also helpful for us to pause and try to better understand their perspective, to be sure that our own bias isn't keeping us from seeing real issues.

2. **Kids become uncomfortable about what they drew.**

   Try this: When my colleague Jeannette and I did this lesson with her fifth graders, we noticed that some of their cheeks went a little blush, and we saw some sheepish grins as we were taking stock of who drew a male or female. We named it and celebrated that they were slowing down to think about their biases, and that it was OK to feel a little awkward—fifth graders appreciate when you just say "awk-ward" in the same tone they use. Knowing you are with them helps put them at ease. This is not an exercise to shame kids; we all have bias.

   It also helps to model what you did when you first tried this stimulus activity. In any class of kids I have used this with, I always share that I fell into the trap of drawing the scientist as a male, or the teacher as a female. "It was my system 1 acting ahead of my system 2!" I explain.

Understanding Microaggressions

Poem Analysis

What Are Microaggressions?

Microaggressions are comments relating to someone's identity that leave a lasting, negative impression on the receiver of the message. As we saw with the group that shared some of these at the beginning of the chapter, they stay with people for a reason. Often, the same microaggressions are heard over and over throughout a person's life.

Why Should We Teach About Microaggressions?

While microaggressions can be intentionally malicious, they are much more likely to come from well-intentioned people who don't fully understand their biases. Microaggressions come from people who want to know more about something or to compliment someone, but don't realize how their words impact the receiver of the message. To avoid microaggressions, people need to know what they are.

The lesson is an exercise in empathy, seeking first to understand how well-intentioned comments relating to a person's identity can weigh on someone over time.

When Should We Teach About Microaggressions?

Teach about microaggressions as soon as or before you hear your students using them. Don't lose the teaching moment. A few typical microaggressions to look out for:

- "Where are you from?" or "What are you?" (Said when someone is focusing on another's ethnic background, especially in a situation when others' backgrounds aren't being discussed)

Are you Spanish?

Are you Chinese?

Are you like Indian from India?

Sorry for what we did to Indians.

Do you know where to get Navajo rugs cheap?

I ♡ your hair

Did you make that?

Native Americans are really into the Earth & spirituality, right?

Oh, like an Indian Princess?

Oh! Like Pocahontas

Did you major in archery?

Are there still Native Americans alive?

Isn't alcoholism a problem in tribes?

- "You're really good at math and science, right?" (Said to kids who are Indian, Pakistani, Chinese, Japanese—or assigned the identity "Asian," encompassing an entire continent and subcontinent made up of dozens of unique countries and cultures)

- "Here, let me do that for you." (Said to a person who someone else has decided is lacking ability, speed, agility, or skill)

- In gym class or on the playground, not picking someone for a team because the chooser assumes they won't be able to win, score, or succeed. (Flashback to the kid who was always picked last—that stays with people)

- Touching hair. (While the intention may be to celebrate its beauty, imagine having people just walk up to you and touch your hair your whole life)

We can also be mindful of our own well-intentioned microaggressions. For example, asking students of color—but not the white students—in your class, "Is anyone home at night to do this homework with?" signals that you have different expectations for those families.

STEP 1: INTRODUCE THE DIANE BURNS POEM "SURE YOU CAN ASK ME A PERSONAL QUESTION"

Before you introduce this poem, read it yourself. You'll see that the poem includes references to "lovers" and to alcoholism. While the poem is strongest as a whole, this lesson still works if you decide not to include those lines in the version you distribute to students.

Have copies of the poem ready to pass out to students. Then, ask them to do a quick turn-and-talk.

> *We are going to read and listen to a poem today from a writer named Diane Burns. I would like you to look at the title. What can you infer from it? Turn and talk.*

Give kids a short time to turn and talk, maybe thirty seconds, and take a few thoughts from the pairs. Kids may notice that the writer is talking to the reader, or sounds conversational. They may say this is going to be about questions.

In this piece of writing, Diane Burns is sharing her experience and her truth. With that come the stereotypes of Native Americans that lead to the microaggressions she is hearing, including the reference to drinking alcohol. It is helpful to be knowledgeable yourself on the historical and cultural context of this specific and burdening stereotype.

Here are some suggested resources for learning more on the topic. A deeper understanding of this stereotype can help you approach it with students.

"American Indians and Alcohol" by Fred Beauvais.
https://pubs.niaaa.nih.gov/publications/arh22-4/253.pdf.

"Your Assumptions About Native Americans and Alcohol Are Wrong" by Elahe Izadi *Washington Post,* February 12, 2016. www.washingtonpost.com/news/post-nation /wp/2016/02/12/your-assumptions-about-native-americans-and-alcohol-are-wrong /?utm_term=.425e9476f44c.

"No, Native Americans Aren't Genetically More Susceptible to Alcoholism: Time to Retire the 'Firewater' Fairytale" by Maia Szalavitz. www.theverge.com/2015 /10/2/9428659/firewater-racist-myth-alcoholism-native-americans.

STEP 2: READ OR LISTEN TO THE POEM

You will be reading the poem aloud. Another option is to use a video of someone reading the poem. A quick online search will yield videos of people—often students—reading this poem. Kids are often engaged when they see and hear a student reading poetry. In a strong reading, the tone of the speaker helps listeners to hear how microaggressions can wear on a person. If you choose to read this aloud, read it aloud to yourself first to hear the voice of the writer. Tell students:

You have a copy of the poem in front of you. As we listen to the poem, you can read along if you'd like. We will hear it twice.

Play the video or read the poem. The kids don't need to do any annotating on the first pass.

STEP 3: WRITTEN REFLECTION

Have students do a written reflection about what they have observed so far.

Thanks for listening. Can you take about two minutes to write down your thoughts on what you have noticed so far in the text? This means that in this time you might be reading the lines of the poem again and writing down your observations. For example, I noticed that it sounds like she is saying "no" a lot.

If kids need prompting, ask, "Can you tell how she feels by the sound of her voice or by the repetition of any language?"

STEP 4: PAIR, SHARE

Transition from the writing by asking everyone to pair up and share with a partner what they noticed in the poem.

Take some ideas from pairs and chart their thinking so far. Encourage them to frame their notes as questions if they are unsure about something: *I wonder why she sounds so annoyed?* or *I wonder what peyote is?* If students haven't come up with the notion that she is answering all the personal questions she is asked, then go ahead and make this observation for them. That is the lens they will need for the second pass through the poem.

> "Microaggressions are the everyday verbal, nonverbal, and environmental slights, snubs, or insults, whether intentional or unintentional, which communicate hostile, derogatory, or negative messages to target persons based solely upon their marginalized group membership."
>
> –Dr. Derald Wing Sue, Columbia University

Noting *who* said *what* on your chart is a great way to allow students to reference other students in either discussion or in writing. Encouraging kids to see themselves and their peers as part of the knowledge library in the classroom is important in the work of social comprehension. It helps kids find allies during difficult conversations—people who can help them work through their ideas and questions on the same or even a different line of thinking.

STEP 5: EXAMINING THE TERM
MICROAGGRESSIONS

Open this discussion by asking, "Has anyone heard the term microaggressions before?" Again, we are not asking if kids know what microaggressions are. We are only asking if they have heard the term.

If you have heard the word before, think about where or when it was. If you haven't heard it before, use the words or parts of a word inside of this term that you may know. Or, perhaps the poem we've been reading might help you to identify what a microaggression is. Turn and talk with someone to see if you can make sense out of it.

Take a few ideas from the group and work together to form a class definition for *microaggression*.

For your own reference, here's my go-to definition of microaggression. It's from Dr. Derald Wing Sue at Columbia University (2010): "Microaggressions are the everyday verbal, nonverbal, and environmental slights, snubs, or insults, whether intentional or unintentional, which communicate hostile, derogatory, or negative messages to target persons based solely upon their marginalized group membership."

As you discuss microaggressions, some kids may have vivid personal experiences they want to discuss or may be wondering if "that one time . . ." was a microaggression. Tell them that if this is the case, they can write about their experience in their journals so they don't forget. There will be an opportunity to share this later in their own writing and/or group discussion.

When kids look at the writer's response to a lifetime of microaggressions, it's easy for them to say, "I can't believe people would ask her such dumb questions!" If you hear this kind of response, it's worth reminding kids that no one is exempt or immune from bias, no matter how well-intentioned or kind we believe we are.

STEP 6: LISTEN TO THE POEM A SECOND TIME
Tell the kids:

> *Let's stretch into some critical thinking and listen to the poem in another way. When we listen this time, try to figure out what questions she is being asked. For example, in the second line, she says: "No, not Chinese." Someone must be asking her for some reason, Are you Chinese?*

As you reread the poem or reshow the video, consider some good pausing points where students can turn and talk.

Charting the questions they think she is being asked is a good way to start building an understanding both of what microaggressions are and of how exhausting continual microaggressions can be for a person.

STEP 7: SHARE AND EXTEND
For kids to really extend this lesson into the world, we can have them consider the target audience for this poem and the writer's message for them. To whom is Diane Burns speaking?

> *Looking at the questions on the chart that we have compiled, I want you to consider all the things she is being asked. And I really think she has been asked them more than once in her life, because writers write from experiences, from "itches they have to scratch," and this seems like something that has been building and bothering her.*
>
> *Take a minute and just write your responses to these thought questions:*
>
> - *Who do you think Diane Burns is speaking to in this piece? (Who is her target audience?)*
> - *What is her tone or attitude, or even message to her audience?*

As students are writing, you can either write down your own thoughts that have perhaps grown out of the rereads you have done or the kid conversations during the lesson. Also make yourself available to anyone who needs extra support by mentioning that you are there to listen or to reread the poem quietly with them.

Have the students move from their cluster in your community space to a circle or a discussion formation in which they can all make eye contact and no one has their back to anyone.

Use a whole-group discussion method that works for your kids. Depending on how we have built our structures together, kids can begin discussion by:

- "Speaking into the silence" —someone just begins with a comment or question, or reads a piece of the text.

- Asking a volunteer to kick it off.

- Beginning with something that I am wondering, which is sometimes different from what I asked students to write about. For this lesson, I may say, "How can we hear this message the author is sending and do better?" Or, "After examining this poem, I am thinking about microaggressions I commit and wondering, how can I do a better job in the world of not making assumptions about others?"

Remember: silence often means thinking time, and it's fine if kids don't jump in right away. There is productive tension in the silence as we are thinking and reflecting. We can remind the kids this feeling signals they are learning.

↑ FOLLOW-UP

The ultimate goals of this lesson are to build an initial understanding of microaggressions and use what we learned from Diane Burns to remember how they can wear over time for the receivers of the message.

Once you've introduced the concept of microaggressions, some of the kids may draw personal connections. Listening to them actively and giving them opportunities to discuss these experiences can deepen their understanding of microaggressions and help them to keep their own sense of self strong. If sharing microaggressions you have heard yourself or even projected onto others feels helpful in connecting to students, do so, but remember to keep the *students'* experiences the focus of these conversations.

This lesson also gives you a foothold for addressing microaggressions if they arise in your classroom community. If you witness or hear about microaggressions, you might confer with the responsible student, asking him or her to consider the effects of their comments.

⇅ ADDRESSING TENSIONS

1. **Students who were not previously familiar with the term** *microaggressions* **suddenly make powerful connections to their own lives.**

   Once we make clear what a microaggression is, kids' lightbulbs may start going off about a time they have said or felt something that sounds like one.

   Try this: Tell kids early on that microaggressions aren't unusual. Tell them about one you have experienced yourself if you are comfortable doing so. Encourage them to write down their experiences so as not to lose their thoughts. Confer with them so you can support them and understand their comfort level in sharing. They may feel empowered to share their experiences with the group at the right time. Or they may just be content with identifying them.

2. **Kids need more examples to "get" microaggressions.**

   Try this: If your group needs more concrete examples after studying what microaggressions might be, share some examples from Dr. Sue:

   - A white man or woman clutches their purse or wallet as a black or Latino man is walking past them. (Message: You and your group are criminals.)
   - You lock the doors in neighborhoods that don't look like yours. (Message: You and your group are criminals.)
   - A female physician with a stethoscope is mistaken for a nurse. (Message: Women should not be in the role of making decisions but rather in a nurturing role, taking direction from the male doctor.)
   - Someone uses the phrase "it was so gay" to describe something they didn't like. (Message: Being gay is negative.)

Refusing to Let Others' Biases Define Us

Identity Statements

What Are Identity Statements?

As students become more comfortable examining their own identities, it is our hope that they are growing the confidence that goes along with affirming them. "I Am" statements are the written statements of affirmation that kids write about themselves. "I am an athlete," for example, or "I am a friend." They are a way for kids to reclaim their identity in case they have ever felt as if certain terms have been assigned to them.

"I Am Not" statements push back against identity labels that others have projected onto kids: "I am not annoying"; "I am not a foreigner."

Why Use "I Am" Statements?

When kids are empowered to announce to the world who they are, it is far less likely that someone else will do it for them. So often in school, kids are being *told* who they are by the language adults use to describe them, by data, or by their own peers. The world assigns or questions our identity constantly, whether explicitly or implicitly: images and headlines tell us who is dangerous and whom we should fear. Ads and social media tell us we aren't fit enough, thin enough, youthful enough, wealthy enough, white enough (see bleaching and whitening products).

We can position kids in such a way that they can and will shout who they are from the rooftops. "I Am" statements can help kids reclaim or reaffirm both their individual identities and the layers of their cultural identities.

When Could "I Am" Statements Be Used?

- After students have done their initial identity webs.
- To encourage positive social media use and healthy image projection.
- In homeroom, advisory periods, and special classes.
- When reading narratives or personal accounts in which the protagonist is judged, labeled, or stereotyped, or is questioning their own identity.
- Whenever you ask the class to revisit their identity webs throughout the year.

STEP 1: REVISIT THE IDENTITY WEBS

Have students get out their original identity webs. Post your web so that students can see it.

> *We are going to revisit our identity webs today. The way we originally created these was by asking ourselves, How do I see myself? Then, without even a second thought, we were able to write, "Well, I am a sister. I am a soccer player." We answered the question with an "I Am" statement. Can you look at your web for just a minute and think about the "I Am" statements that are hiding in your web? Watch me as I do this.*

I point to my web and the word *athlete*. Then, I say aloud: "I AM an athlete." I point to the next phrase, *daughter of Indian Muslim immigrants,* while saying, "I AM the daughter of Indian Muslim immigrants."

> *This one is not always easy for me to say because it is connected to negative stereotypes about Muslims, but I wanted to share one I feel proud of even though it is hard to share with total confidence. I will share more with you about that one in a minute.*

Be intentional with the examples you choose. I purposely go for these two because one is a connection to almost every student in my class and the other is a topic that makes me feel a little vulnerable, but I own that and say it aloud for them.

STEP 2: AFFIRM WHO WE ARE

Have students first point quietly to two words or phrases on their webs that they can turn into "I Am" statements. This allows for some thinking time.

> *Can you try what I just did? Point to something on your web that you can say with confidence.*

Then have them turn to a partner and share one or two of their "I Am" statements. Your role here is to mingle and listen to what they are saying. What parts of their identity are they gravitating to first? What is comfortable? If you can, lean in and ask a few kids to share when the group comes back together.

Bring them back to share.

> *Anyone have one that they went for right away? One that they can shout from the rooftops!? I heard lots and even spoke with a few of you.*

Take a few responses. In my experience, the sharing by the first few kids gives everyone else courage, and all of a sudden everyone wants to share. They may be slow to start, but once kids hear a few brave friends, they will give it a go. In cases where everyone wants to share, I catch the moment and do a quick go-around, or carousel, letting each kid offer their statements. If you find the same energy in your classroom, it's worth trying. If not, don't feel that you have to force it. Here are a few I heard recently in Ben Charpartier's fourth-grade classroom at NIST International School:

I am a good friend.

I am Japanese and Nepali and American.

I am a gamer.

I am a gymnast.

Affirm what all kids have shared before moving on. I might say something as simple as:

> *Awesome! Thanks for sharing how you identify, everyone!*

STEP 3: MODEL: NAMING IDENTITIES THAT HAVE BEEN ASSIGNED TO US

Introduce the idea of identities that are assigned to us.

> *This next part may feel a little different. Using our web that we now have in front of us, I want you to consider something: What pieces of our identity have been assigned to us by others? By "assigned to us," I mean things we have heard said directly to us, things we may feel from making observations out in the world, messages or times people either*

unintentionally or intentionally hurt us by showing that they have biases that affect us. Remember the time we talked about microaggressions— those comments people make that communicate a negative message to us? Those conversations we have had that don't sit well with us, or stay with us, and we aren't always sure why? Those are times when we might feel that someone is assigning an identity to us.

Tape your web to the center of a larger sheet of paper.

I am going to think this one out in front of you, so listen in, even though I know some of you may already be thinking about the ways people tried to tell you who you are or commented on some part of your identity.

With a different color marker than you used in the first web, use the space around your original web to write words that you have been called or labeled, words that you have internalized from what you have heard, read, and seen in society.

I encourage you to be bold in your choices. At this point in the lesson, I have taken my marker and written "terrorist." Yes, I go for it. We are focusing on being candid in this chapter.

When I do this, kids sometimes respond immediately, before I can say something about it. "What?!" they blurt out. "You, Ms. Ahmed!?!" or they have uncomfortable smiles on their faces just because the word *terrorist* has such a current and heavy stigma. To head this off, I have begun talking through *as* I write the word; they can see me make my thinking visible to them. This eliminates any dramatic silence, which tended to make my example too much about me.

As I write the word *terrorist* I am talking:

This is the first word I am writing because it is affecting my heart right now. Ever since 9/11, an event where some extremists with names similar to my surname, Ahmed, took down the World Trade Center in New York City by hijacking planes, I have felt this label has been assigned to me. And not only me—an entire group of millions of people in America who had nothing to do with the terrorist attack that day have also been called terrorists.

Keep moving. If someone sounds like they want to have a talk with you on the spot about what you've written, offer to do it another time, so as not to take away from the focus of this lesson. Quickly kid watch, noticing their faces, body language, or even subtle commentary. If you see discomfort, you might say, "I can see some of you reacting to this. Hold on to those thoughts and if you want to talk

Figure 3.2 A new layer on my identity web

about them with me later, we can. But right now I am going to keep going so you have time to try this too."

Choose another item to add, and continue. Next, I write *small* and keep talking.

> *Many people have called me short, "shorty," or little, or have assumed I can't reach the overhead luggage bin in a plane. Often, they have done so with what they think are good intentions or in a kidding manner, but I've heard it enough I think.* (I say this with a smile.) *I am not little, I am strong!*

Then, transition back to the kids and their webs.

> *Thanks for listening to me; now I am going to give you some time to consider this outer web yourself. The place where identity has been assigned to you.*

STEP 4: KIDS NAME IDENTITIES THAT HAVE BEEN ASSIGNED TO THEM

Let the kids know that they'll be going back to their seats or an independent work space to do some thinking and writing on their own. There are two ways that kids can do this. One, have a big sheet of paper for each kid and use that to create an outer web like I did in my modeling. Another way is to use sticky notes. Kids just attach the notes around the outside of their webs rather than using paper. Think about where the webs will "live" after this lesson—that may help you decide.

> *OK, this next part I am going to have you do on your own rather than talking with anyone just yet. It took me some time to think about this by myself before I could talk with you and write it.*
>
> *On your tables are papers that are big like the one I have up here and also some tape. When you go back to your seats, you can tape your web right in the middle of it. Then start to really think the way I just did in front of you and add the identity labels you have been assigned to the outside of your web.*

If they need prompting, you can project the thinking questions:

- What identity has been assigned to you?
- What words or labels or phrases have you heard about any groups you identify with in your life?
- What comments or messages have stayed with you, even if you thought that friends or others were just playing around at the time?

Before sending the kids to work, offer them the option to stay with you on the rug.

> *If you need extra support on how to think through this, stay here. Otherwise go to a space where you can work without distraction.*
> *Also, remember that this thinking is private to you. Let's respect that about everyone in the room. You will have five to eight minutes for this depending on how you are working.*

This time, while students are writing, is valuable. As you kneel beside each kid, be aware that they are trying to wrap their heads around something they may never have let themselves think about before, something that they have pushed far back in their minds. If you confer, you can lean in and ask them about what they are thinking. Did any stories that you shared connect to any experiences they've had?

Watch the room, looking for movement or inaction: Are they able to write right away? Are they still taping the paper? Are they hiding their writing? Are they sitting with blank paper, absent from the writing and thinking? Are they leaning over, writing vigorously?

Bring students' attention back to a central meeting point. They can watch you from where they are sitting.

STEP 5: CREATE OUR IDENTITY STATEMENTS

Model how to write "I Am" and "I Am Not" statements:

> *We had a lot of energy when we were able to proclaim to the world, "I am!"*
> *Then the energy changed a little when I talked through why some labels*
> *have been assigned to me and when you tried it on your own. That is*
> *totally OK; putting tough stuff out there is never easy or fun. Sometimes*
> *it changes our tone or mood and our body language.*
>
> *You guys, we are going to try to conquer that negative feeling right*
> *now by proclaiming and reclaiming our identity. We are going to take*
> *it back from all the people who say we are something we aren't and tell*
> *people who we are!*
>
> *I have some strips of paper up here that I am going to fill out for you.*
> *Watch me as I write some "I Am" statements on them.*

Have a pile of sentence strips—long pieces of paper or cardstock—ready for kids to use.

On one strip, write something that you identify as:

> *I am an athlete.*

On a second strip, write an identity that others have given you that you refute:

> *I am NOT a terrorist.*

Then, move on to a third strip:

> *And I'll do one more. This is the one that helps me reclaim a piece of my*
> *identity. I get to reverse that "I Am Not" statement by really owning*
> *who I am and being proud of it. After I wrote my "I Am Not" statement,*
> *I wondered, "OK, what do I identify as that will refute or counter that*
> *label? How do I correct those who have said I was something I am not?*

> *I am the daughter of Indian Muslim immigrants.*

Post the stems of these statements where students can see them:

- I am . . .
- I am not . . .

Invite kids to try this work for themselves.

> *Do you think you can do this? Write strips that begin with I am . . . and*
> *I am not . . . . You have a lot of resources with you to help: your original*

*web, your new outer web, the stories and experiences you remembered,
and all of us. This is a great time to move toward working with a buddy if
you would like to. I am so much more empowered when I can talk through
difficult things with someone else after I do my own writing and thinking.*

*You can pick any color strip, any marker, and write it in your own
unique way. It just has to be legible. You can make more than one of each
kind of statement, but go for writing at least one of each if you can.*

When I was working in Ben's classroom, Ben noticed that some of his kids
needed extra support before they could begin. So, he modeled writing his statements for the kids this way:

*For my "I Am" statement, I'm going to write, "I am a third-culture kid."
This is a phrase that I just learned this past year actually. It means that
I spent most of my life living outside of the country and culture where
my parents and my passport are from. That has greatly affected my
identity and I think about it all the time.*

*For my "I Am Not" statement, I'm thinking about how the kids
of the country I moved to always called me names to remind me
I was an outsider, like the character Fez from an old show called
That '70s Show.*

He adds "I am not an outsider, or a foreigner, I am not Fez" to the
outside of his web in front of the kids.

Seeing what their teacher—someone they have built a bond with—was
thinking instilled more confidence in the kids and provided a nudge for
the few who needed it.

STEP 6: SHARE AND GO PUBLIC

Bring students back together to close the loop on identity statements and
brainstorm how to go public.

*Before we decide how we want to go public with our statements, I want
to make sure we are clear about the difference between personal identity
and stereotypes.*

*Personal identity is how we see ourselves: ethnicity, gender and
gender identity, religion, sexual orientation, ability. Those things we feel
strongly about and can declare with confidence.*

But the labels? The things that were assigned to us, the words we took back? Those are stereotypes and assumptions that other people made about us based on their own beliefs and bias and without getting to know us first. You with me?!

OK, let's brainstorm the best way to celebrate our statements!

Ask students where they want these statements to go. Here are a few ways I've seen kids and teachers go public with these statements:

- Hang the statements on an "I Am" wall. In *Upstanders*, Smokey Daniels and I highlight a teacher, Ambra Johnson, who invites the entire grade level to make "I Am" statements to hang on an "I Am" wall.

- Make a video. In the past I have had students make a PSA-style video to say who they were.

- Post the statements around the school. Some kids have wanted to hang them by their lockers or in their advisories.

- Discuss them in your classroom space. Bring all the statements to the rug to share.

- Create a writing piece from them. In Ben's classroom, for example, students wrote about their identity.

- Do a gallery walk. Spread the statements out on tables and let students do a "gallery walk" to read them and leave sticky notes with comments of support. Then, as a class, kids discuss what they notice. Just as in any situation where people might comment on someone else's ideas

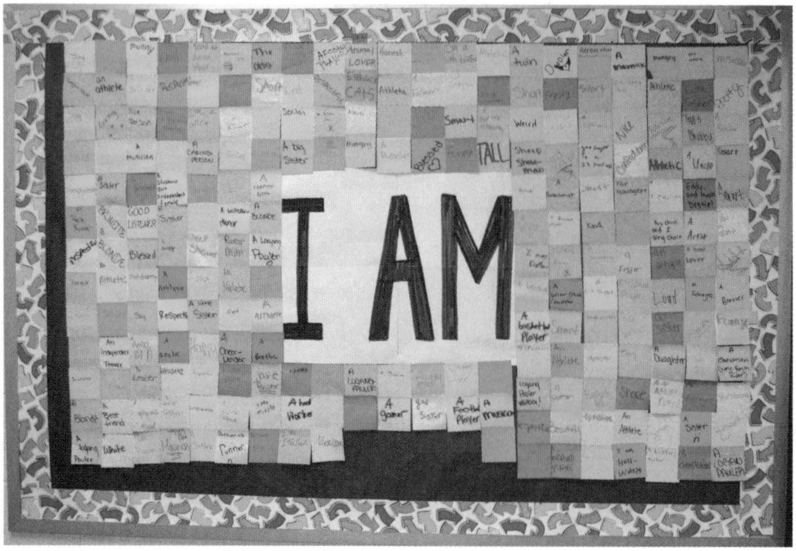

Figure 3.3 To begin the school year, eighth-grade teacher Amy Hicks and her students created an "I Am" wall to tell the world who they are.

that have been put out into the world, support students in how to do this well. Students are likely familiar with social media platform comments and "likes." So an engaging way to look at a conversation on these strips could be one that kids are familiar with: the thumbs up, thumbs down, and hearts we see in social media feedback on YouTube, Instagram, Twitter, Facebook, and Tumblr. Before the gallery walk, talk to students about why they use these when they do. A conversation around whether a thumbs down is ever appropriate might be a good place to start.

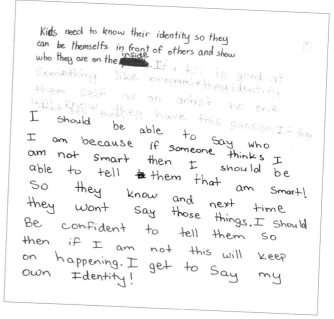

Figure 3.4 After this lesson, fourth graders wrote about their identity.

↑ FOLLOW-UP

When kids hear messages society sends them over and over, they can start to believe them. There is a danger that labels infiltrate our own definition of ourselves because it [the definition] has been assaulted so often. Supporting kids in naming what they know themselves to be—even, or especially, when they are feeling unsure of themselves—can give them strength. And really, it is magical to watch how assured they are and the smiles they project when they can confidently say who they are in a safe space. We do this work in the hope that they can remember this feeling in a not-so-safe space or in a difficult conversation in their lives outside of school.

The audience for this lesson is not only us and the kids. Making their statements public will have a ripple effect. It begins a conversation in a visible space, much like visual art, allowing others to take in, reflect, connect, and then pay it forward. The biggest impact I have seen is that when statements are posted publicly, other communities then take on the challenge, creating and sharing their own statements. When we look openly and honestly at our webs we unpack our identity in candid ways. Allowing kids to get these statements out may teach us something about some of the messages we are sending them about their identity as well.

⇅ ADDRESSING TENSIONS

1. **Students say they have nothing to write outside of their web.**

   Students may say they have nothing to write because they think that their comments must be something heavy, like my terrorist example. In other cases, kids may say they have nothing to write because they do not feel safe sharing something that may be intensely personal. And some students, like one we witnessed in Ben's class ("no one has ever said anything mean to me or made me feel bad about myself") actually claim they have nothing to write about because they unknowingly have been in the privileged position of just being "normal" (which, to this student, meant able-bodied, blonde, blue-eyed, athletic, good-looking, smart, and nice).

   Try this: Obviously, we are not trying to force a student to retrieve times where someone made them feel bad about themselves or to share something they do not feel safe revealing. Instead, try asking this question: "What is something that no one knows about you?" I tried that with a student once who had "nothing to write," and he answered by saying, "I don't know! Everyone just thinks I am quiet and nice and maybe weird because I don't say much." This gave me a starting point. I asked: "Have people told you you're weird?" "No," he responded, "but they don't always approach me because I keep to myself. I am actually a really loyal friend, ya know?" We added *loyal* on the inside of his web. Then we brainstormed how people may view him if they aren't approaching him. He came up with *quiet* and *weird*. His statements were:

   - I am loyal.
   - I am not quiet (if you get to know me).

Synthesis: Making Thinking Visible

When we put ourselves in a place where we are candid and real, where we make the implicit explicit, we can move forward in our commitment to social comprehension. However, the old saying that "honesty is the best policy" never reveals the complexities of self-examination that have to happen in the process of self-disclosure.

In this chapter, students have done some serious work: they held up a mirror to their identities, looked for their own bias, addressed microaggressions, and took a stand to reclaim their identity from others who might try to strip it away.

Again, ask students to revisit their "At First I Thought . . . Now I Think" journals, adding new sheets as necessary. Of course, you don't have to wait for these reminders to ask students to revisit these journals—ask them to update their notes whenever it seems appropriate. The journal works best when it is a scrapbook of their journey through social comprehension, not an exercise they turn in for credit.

Let's look back and see where their thinking has shifted, and ask them to continue journaling their growth.

> We have come a long way together and I am watching your minds and hearts grow a little stronger every day. You're critically thinking through reading, media, and discussions; you've listened to others and you've been candid with yourself. None of that is easy.
>
> I want to revisit those same journal pages you worked on earlier. It might be great to read what you wrote the last time, on what you have learned about yourself that you didn't know before. That way when you add on, you won't feel like you are repeating anything but can build off of those thoughts.
>
> We have focused so much on the idea of being candid and honest with ourselves about how we view others and how others have viewed us. We've dug further into an inquiry into the self—the toughest kind, really.
>
> What do you continue to learn about yourself? What is something new that you have learned from someone else, either a stranger or someone in this class? Did anyone change your mind on something? Were there times when you listened simply to understand and not to reply?

Remember, this is your journal. It is for your eyes and ours if we confer together. How you share outside of that is up to you. You make the choice on how you jot down your thoughts—sketching, bulleting, typing and taping them in, writing—be creative!

The goal in returning to this journal across the year is, first, to help students to see and track changes in their thinking over time. Second, by revisiting the journal page at multiple points during the year, we can help make the simple yet powerful practice of reflecting on new learning and self-discovery part of students' personal tools for social comprehension.

4

Becoming Better Informed

My advisory is beginning its day with a soft start. Some of the kids are playing Scrabble. Others are reading the paper. But Julian isn't smiling this November morning. Disengaged from the group, he leans against the whiteboard, playing with the marker caps.

As I begin reading daily announcements, he suddenly calls out, "Ms. Ahmed! There was another bombing last night, I said!" The boom of his voice brings me to a pause, brings us all to a pause. He normally speaks in soft, low tones. It alerts me to the fact that he has already tried to tell me this, and I missed it. I realize that I've made a mistake—I've started talking school without really paying attention to how my kids were beginning the day.

"I read that last night, Julian. Do you want to talk about it?"

Julian's questions come out in a rush. "Is it going to happen to us (New York City) again? Are we safe uptown since we aren't near that area (World Trade Center site/ Financial District)?"

"I would consider us safe, yes. But it depends how you feel, if you feel safe."

Julian pauses, then continues. "I am not sure. I just don't understand why it keeps happening. Why certain people and cities are attacked. How many times have we been attacked? When was the last time before 9/11?"

The other students start to chime in with their own questions and comments:

Yeah, I read that; who was it?

Man, no one is going to bomb us up here. We aren't near anything important.

What bombing? I didn't hear about a bombing.

Why do people want to bomb other people—like, do they want to bomb Puerto Ricans and Dominicans too?

I heard it was Muslim terrorists; is that what they believe in or something?

I write down their questions as they talk so they know their questions are important to all of us and because I want to make sure I understand what they are asking. I reassure the kids that these are all legitimate worries and questions and that later, we can talk this out and try to find some answers for the questions that are on their minds.

Julian nods. "Sorry I yelled; I just didn't sleep last night because I was worried. I guess it is just in my news this morning, ya know."

Before the first bell rings in the morning, all of our students are coming to school with their own news. Sometimes it is news from home, other times from an event they had over the weekend or something that just happened at school, and at times it is news of the world on their minds. Students' news can be any topic, event, feelings, or pieces of information that they have on their mind and will most likely carry with them all day.

We are quick to get busy *doing school* when kids arrive. Getting them to class on time, prepared, with as little friction as possible. Then we ask them to be quiet, polite, sit still, and listen for the next seven hours. When we neglect the myriad of news that is coming through the door with them or listen with an inauthentic sincerity (they can see right through this), we are ignoring factors that may impede their ability to learn and engage with their day. We are also missing an important opportunity to teach social comprehension.

Let's look again at some of the comments and questions from that morning in my classroom, and the assumptions I hear forming as they speak their truths.

Man, no one is going to bomb us up here. We aren't near anything important.

What I was hearing: Where we live isn't valuable.

I heard it was Muslim terrorists; is that what they believe in or something?

What I was hearing: Do all people who believe in Islam believe in terrorism?

Now, consider what kinds of beliefs can take root if we don't provide opportunities for kids to become better informed, if we leave them to ponder these questions with only their assumptions as their guides, and offer no time to mitigate their fears with knowledge.

To help students get beyond initial assumptions and build their social comprehension, we need to make time for and apply what Peter Johnston (2012) calls "knowledge construction"—an emphasis on a dynamic theory about knowledge, uncertainty, a consideration of context, and different perspectives. If we are fixed about how we feel and have little capacity to move from that mind-set, there will be no movement in dialogue, and little growth. We need classrooms that honor risky questions and nudge kids to ask about their identity and the news inquiries that adults (whose absolute beliefs have set in) have a hard time making.

Johnston argues that in dialogic classrooms, "where there are lots of open questions and extended exchanges among students" (2012, 52), kids are valued as the constructors of knowledge. Through their questions, disagreements, and dialogue, they can negotiate meaning from multiple perspectives, including their own. I humbly add that if we value identity and honor kids' news, then strategize with them on how to muddle through the self-exploration and collaborative dialogue that incidentally occurs with all the questions they have, we will grow a generation that honors a range of perspectives and flexibility of thought.

Currently, there is little room for asking questions in school if you are the student. Students are in the business of answering adult-engineered questions; rarely are they doing the asking, or working through how to craft questions they want answers to, especially as they climb the grades. Or if they are, they aren't given the time to answer them. I, for one, have been guilty of teaching the lesson where my objective is

Through their questions, disagreements, and dialogue, they can negotiate meaning from multiple perspectives, including their own.

to have kids ask all the questions they can and excitedly affix them to our beautiful shared chart—a sticky note graveyard, where their questions are laid to rest, never given the time to be explored.

Can we push forward from student-centered to socially minded classrooms? Where dynamic student questions set us on a journey of shaping our individual and shared social comprehension?

Can we commit to the idea that kids have the ability to initiate topics worth exploring with their news?

The lessons in this chapter make this practice visible in the classrooms. We can invite students to share their news, to consider how their news relates to their identity, and to gather a more informed understanding of their news.

Kids like Julian come to school with the weight of the world on their shoulders. He can't do history in class today if he is concerned about his community right now. My hope is that the lessons in this chapter enable us to help students better understand what is weighing on them, and either lay that weight down or learn how to bear it with greater strength and purpose. We can do this by listening to them, legitimizing their questions, and carving out time to send the message that their news matters.

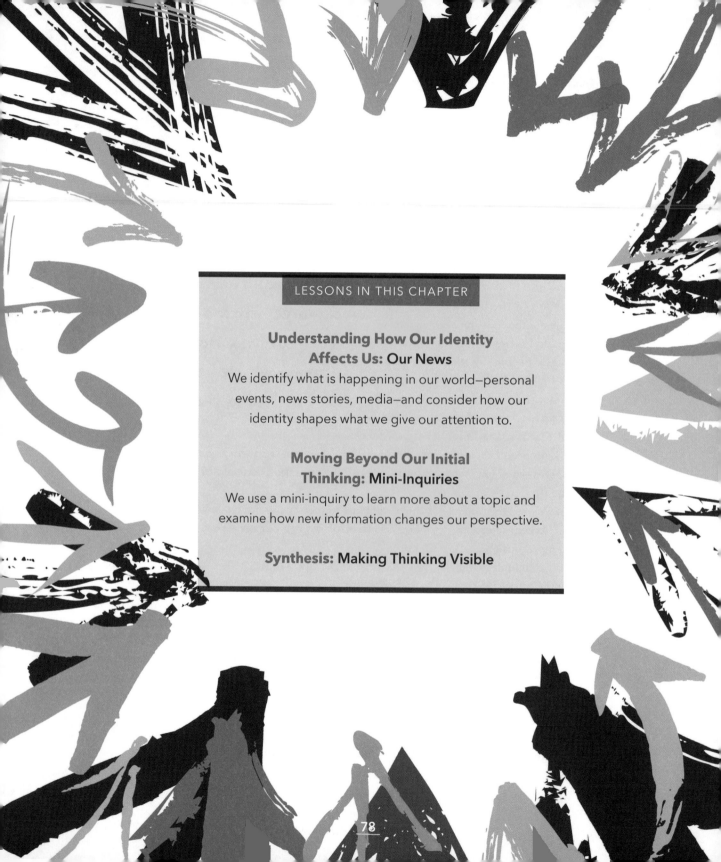

Understanding How Our Identity Affects Us

Our News

What Is Our "News"?

As stated previously, a person's "news" can be any topic, event, feelings, or pieces of information that they have on their mind and will most likely carry with them all day. This lesson is designed to give kids the time and space to investigate the questions they have about their news. It does not necessarily mean the news media is the source of what is happening, but sheds a light on what our students see as news in their lives and supports them in thinking through their questions about it.

Why Do We Talk to Kids About What's in Their News?

Kids' news gives us immediate, relevant opportunities for practicing the skills of social comprehension. More importantly, examining it with kids helps them to make sense of their world.

When Do We Ask Kids What's in Their News?

- When the world hands us a curriculum the night before—that is, anything that is shared publicly on social platforms that we expect will be on kids' minds: attacks, shootings, politics, breaking sports news, parades, rallies, marches, protests, notable deaths shared far and wide.

- When kids want to know more about a topic that is new, important, or that they "heard about" somewhere.

- When there is any measure of crisis at school, as a way to address the issue without artificially smoothing it over. We can take time for the class to pause and slow down, and give support to anyone who urgently needs it.

- When we are asking kids to formulate an opinion, take a stance, or craft writing under the mode of opinion: essays, reviews, debates, speeches, letters.

STEP 1: CONSIDER WHAT "NEWS" IS IN OUR WORLD

Set the stage for kids to consider what we call news. Here's how I might do this with a class:

> When you log in to any social media, such as Twitter, Facebook, Instagram, or YouTube, there is always a newsfeed. It is people we follow, whether we know them personally or not, telling us what is in their "news." A new baby or pet, a new job, winning a game, their weekend or vacation photos, a new book or article they are reading, something that happened in politics they think we should know about.
>
> Because you have done such incredible work on identity, you are becoming experts on your own identities and how to build connections with others about their identities. Now we are ready to begin exploring how our identity—our families, experiences, friends, who we follow, where we live—informs the way we respond to the "newsfeed" out in the world.

Model for students how you'll make notes about your own news in your journal. Fold or draw a T-chart for students to see on the left page of the notebook spread, leaving the right side of the notebook blank for now—we'll use it later in this lesson.

Label the left side of the T-chart "What's in My News?" Label the right side of the chart "My Thinking." I might explain what I'm doing by saying:

> On the left side of this chart, we are going to list all the things that are in our own news or current events right now that matter to us. This is where we'll list what is happening within our class, our school, our city, or our own world.
>
> Then, on the right side, we are going to list all our personal thoughts on this topic—what our questions are, any opinions we may have, our ideas, even worries. I am going to show you how I do this on my chart; then you'll do your own.

Ask students to set up this same chart in their journals.

Next, think aloud as you fill in the columns on the chart. Here's how I might think out loud for students in making the chart below.

> So, something in my news is the ban on heading in youth soccer for kids under the age of ten.
>
> I read an article about it and at first I was bothered by it because we were taught to head the ball safely, and it was a big part of the game growing up. I am even going to write here, I love headers! I even scored a couple goals off headers! To me that is part of the game. But then I started coaching, and I've talked to referees about this rule. Can it really be that unsafe? I am going to come back to this one.
>
> Another type of ban that is on my mind is the current ban on travelers from certain countries that are predominantly Muslim. The way it is being laid out by our government and the response covered in our media make me so tense. I worry about many members of my family who travel often, including me. But I need to know more about the reasons for the ban; I am uninformed about the data and reasons. I have more questions than answers.

What's in My News?	My Thinking *(questions, opinions, ideas, emotions)*
Heading ban in US Youth Soccer	I love headers! I was taught how to head the ball when I was very young. We would spend so much time on this at practice. I have scored a few goals off headers! Is it really that unsafe?
The Muslim Ban/immigration policy headlines	This affects many people in my life. It upsets me to no end, the way people view family members that I love. Can something like this be legal?
Cooking at home or going out to eat	
Need new running shoes/half marathon training	

The amount of the chart that I fill out depends on the learners I have in front of me. Some classes need more modeling than others. I do this in an authentic way, meaning I won't write something that is not truly in my news. As a general rule, news on the minds of my kids is on my mind as well. The kids are constantly in my news.

During my think-aloud, I'll try to show as much of a balanced perspective as I can, modeling for students how they can think about a more charged topic in their news. For example, when adding the note about the Muslim ban, I might try this:

This piece of my news has stayed with me because I get upset and frustrated by it. I need to give it more time so I understand it better and then do something about it, if that is what it calls for.

STEP 2: STUDENTS JOT ABOUT WHAT'S IN THEIR NEWS

After modeling, give students an opportunity to try the chart on their own:

That was my newsfeed. Things that are on my mind and that I am thinking about. Some of it is really personal. I feel a range of emotions, and I think that is important to think about too. For the things that I really needed to work through, I showed my thinking in a question. I did this because I want to find out more. This will help me feel a little more settled, I think.

Try a quick turn-and-talk with someone about what may be in your news. Thirty seconds each; go!

Listen in here and watch. Who is talking? Who isn't? The kids who are quiet may be the ones you support first during independent work time.

Do you think you could try this on your own? List as many things you can think of that are in your news right now. You may end up using your identity web for this, so have that handy. Once you list your news, think about why it is in your news. How do you feel about it?

Use my chart to help you. If you think you can go off and do this independently, off you go to a space to work; if not, stay with me and I can model a couple more or work through your first ones with you.

Some of them may have already started while you were modeling, because kids are naturally and constantly looking for connections to what you are saying.

If kids stay with you, it may take only a simple prompt, like "What's going on this week or weekend for you?" to activate some ideas. When we know our kids intimately, it's easier to ask them something specific to get them started: "How's karate going? Do you have a recital coming up? What game are you trying to beat right now? How's the collecting going?"

When you get to move about the room, kneel down or lean in with the intent to listen and extend their thinking about their news if they need it.

STEP 3: TURN AND TALK
Once kids have had a few minutes on their own with this work, ask them to share their notes with a partner near them.

Why don't you turn and talk to a partner about how you filled in your news? Be sure to listen as well. Their thinking box may help you think too, and you can add more to your feed. I also know that when I try and explain to someone what I am thinking, just saying it out loud helps me clarify my thoughts.

STEP 4: MODEL HOW YOUR NEWS CONNECTS TO YOUR IDENTITY
Displaying both the "in my news" notes you made earlier in the lesson and your identity web helps the kids to see how our identities influence our news.

Thanks for sharing with someone near you. I know I asked you to have your webs too. Earlier when you were writing, I noticed that I can trace my news directly back to my web. What is "in my news" is unique to my identity.

I point to something on my "What's in my news?" feed and connect it to my web. Then I ask them to consider how their identities relate to their news.

This whole thing here about headers in soccer (I point to my identity web and my news) *is because I have been playing my whole life and I am so interested in how the game is changing.*

I am going to add a new column to my chart to give me a place to write about how my news is connected to my identity. I am going to write soccer player *and* coach *in the identity column because how I identify affects what I think about this topic.*

I don't know about you, but understanding how our news is related to our identity gives me a new perspective, or way of seeing things. To be honest, sometimes I see things that people care about and I catch myself wondering how anyone could possibly care about the things they're sharing. But the more I consider what is in my news next to my identity web, the more I realize that my identity affects how I respond to the world around me, the same way the things I find silly or don't connect to are important in someone else's news. It may not matter to me, but it absolutely matters to them and their identity, or it wouldn't be in their news. And I need to do a better job of understanding and empathizing with that.

Show students that you are adding two more columns on the right side of your existing chart. Label the first of these new columns *My Identity*. Leave the heading of the final column blank for now. You should now have a four-column chart with the following headings:

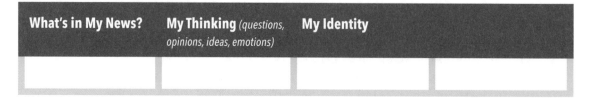

What's in My News?	My Thinking *(questions, opinions, ideas, emotions)*	My Identity	

STEP 5: STUDENTS CONSIDER HOW THEIR NEWS CONNECTS TO THEIR IDENTITY

Right where they are, have students scan their T-chart and identity webs to find the connections between their news and their identities. Then, ask them to use the new column of their chart to note which aspects of their identity are related to each news item. You may still have a few kids who are not seeing any connection to the topic on the list or finding it difficult to transfer the connection to the topic.

I may think through a few more on my chart for the kids who stay and for others who went back to their seats, but are still peeking up for a little help.

STEP 6: SHARE

Give students an opportunity to share their news, their thinking about how they feel, what they wonder, and the connections they've found to their identity. Recognize that some kids have things they want to keep private. Before the share, ask students to decide what they want to keep private for now, and what they might share.

> *Thanks for sharing your news feeds with us today. I wanted to really think about all the things we observe, hear, watch, and take part in in our lives, and give us space to dig deeper into how we feel about them and what we are wondering that we need answered. Your identity and your experiences really help create what is on your newsfeed: it is unique to you. Some of the things on our feed might just be opinions or emotions for now, but by slowing down and showing our thinking through questions, we can develop a better understanding of things that, for now, feel too big or confusing. For things like immigration policies and the Muslim ban, there may be people who feel differently than I do. But all I can do is stay informed and ask more questions, gaining some perspective so that I am able to talk and listen to others. I still have the right to be upset, but having more information and more time to think about it will help me understand why it feels the way it does to me and to others.*
>
> *The next steps are an action plan so this chart is a living, breathing doc just like our identity webs. We can use it to think of next steps to find out more, feel more, do more, learn more, and grow from our questions.*

↑ FOLLOW-UP

As an add-on to this lesson, you can chart what kids are stating as their news during the share or create a chart where they post it themselves. If you are in the habit of noticing where identity hides in our everyday choices and work, you can direct kids to take note of the class newsfeed. What does it say about individuals and you as a community? Keep the newsfeed chart alive in your classroom by revisiting it, using it as a source for mini-inquiry topics, and adding to it as the year goes on. Keeping students' news prominent in the classroom reminds them that what they value matters.

This lesson gives us a foundation to work from when we encounter disagreements in our classroom or situations when students are surprised, hurt, or angered by a peer's opinion on a topic. In these situations, we can also remind students of the link between identity and our news (what we notice, value, and think about), and consider how we can be respectful of others' identities, values, and experiences.

⇅ ADDRESSING TENSIONS

1. **Students have "no news" to write down.**

   Try this: The topics the class discusses in this lesson don't need to be headlines or tragic news—they could be anything that invites talk around school, in your class, or in the media. If individual students don't respond to prompts such as, "What happened in your life in the last week?" or "What's something you've seen in the news recently?" give them time to read student-friendly sources, like *Time for Kids*, *New York Times Upfront*, Newsela, *HuffPost Teen*, and *Teen Vogue*. Common Sense Media's list of news sources for kids (www .commonsensemedia.org/lists/best-news-sources-for-kids#) is also a great resource. Carving out a time in class to read appropriate articles helps keep everyone informed while still letting them choose what they deem as news. This will look different in every grade level and every school. In general, look for topics that appeal to kids' innate superpowers: an acute sense of justice, keen observation, and big hearts absorbing everything happening around them.

2. **Kids believe that they "know" a great deal about a topic that they have no personal experience or identity connection with, or what they "know" may be an opinion that offends others in the room.**

   For example, one student's news may expose their anti-same-sex-marriage views, while another student may have same-sex parents.

   Try this: Proactively, while kids are working, try to get a read on *all* the news in the class so that you know where there may be potential conflicts. However, do not censor what kids write: the work of social comprehension involves candor and difficult conversations.

   Situations like these are the reason we spend so much time in Chapter 1 getting to know ourselves and others in our learning community. You can't avoid every tension that may arise. So, we need to take great care of each other during the work of social comprehension.

If a student shares his or her beliefs directly and it negatively impacts the identity of another, consider the following as you decide how to respond:

- What have students just shared or heard from one another?
- What feelings have been acknowledged? (Do both students know that someone's identity is at stake?)
- How can you support the student who is working toward becoming more informed and also the student(s) whose identity is now vulnerable or diminished?

Giving students time to write or discuss is one strategy that works. Revisit the language or agreements of your community in having difficult conversations from Chapter 2, and the lesson on bias in Chapter 3 to help move forward.

3. **The news that kids have does not seem "controversial" or "important" enough to you.**

There may be kids whose lists include only their volleyball tournament, an upcoming concert, and the student council election. That is OK. Don't push them to add a current news topic. Don't negate the importance of that volleyball game just because it isn't connected to your identity. Social comprehension involves actively calling out bias, even our own. Many of us have a vested interest in the social and political atmosphere in our out-of-school lives. We read, write, march, protest, speak, donate, attend, tweet—we take some form of action for the things we care about. But we have to be very mindful of regulating our bias and checking our personal crusader capes at the door so as not to bring only the issues we care about to the front of the room.

When striving toward social comprehension, we want to err on the side of being more informed than uninformed. Obvious? Yes, but conviction clouds the distinction between an informed versus uninformed opinion when conversations carry an emotional charge.

Try this: If promoting agency and voice in our kids is a goal, we need to remember to ask and hear what is in their news. Most times, that news points straight back to their identity. So, asking them what is in their news sends the message that we will mentor them in reading more, writing through, and speaking up and out for topics and issues that matter to them, first.

Rather than insisting that students focus on topics that we see as important, ask questions to show you care and want to find out why the things they've chosen are at the heart of their news. What are the feelings that have pushed this news to the forefront of this student's mind? I once had a student mention an upcoming volleyball game in her news. Rather than brushing this off as not controversial enough, I tried to get at the heart of why it was in her news. We zeroed in on her emotions, which led her to examine a piece of her identity: she was nervous and really anxious about her performance and about having a friend on the opposing team. Learning more about why she included her volleyball game showed that the student was focusing on issues that were deeply important to her, even if her initial phrasing made the subject seem light. It turned out to be a highly productive conference. We tried to form a question around her worries: *Will we still be friends no matter who wins or loses? What if we don't talk?* We came up with an action plan that she would smile and high-five her friend before the game for good luck and make a promise with her friend then and there to do it after the game no matter what. In navigating her news, she was doing some social problem solving on the spot!

Suggested Resource Stack for Newsfeeds

Newsfeeds from trending social media such as Twitter, Facebook, Instagram, and YouTube channels expose us to what is in someone's news and what they are thinking and wondering around it.

Professional news sources can also give kids a starting place for identifying what resonates with them. A few periodicals in particular:

The Week

New York Times Upfront

Scholastic News

Time for Kids

National Geographic (adult and kid versions)

Teen Vogue

Faces

Moving Beyond Our Initial Thinking

Mini-Inquiries

What Does It Mean to Move Beyond Our Initial Thinking?

This is a continuation of the previous lesson on our personal news. Once kids have listed what is in their news and begin to be candid about how they feel, they will choose what piece of news they want to explore further and ask some hard questions: *What are the gaps in my knowledge? What action will I take? How can I grow from this?*

My News	My Thinking (questions, opinions, ideas, emotions)	My Identity	My Ideas for Action
#MuslimBan Islamophobia	• What can I do to protect my parents? (Should I write a letter?) • What resources do I need for classroom work? • Mom goes to churches to spread knowledge over fear - so Proud & Inspiring!	• Daughter of Muslim • Immigrants / American citizens • Muslim families in school (Teacher) • Writer · Aunt • Speaker · Niece • Suburban Kid	• Find range of news articles), OP-Eds. • Study a map of banned countries • Talk w/ someone who is affected by this ban = real people • Look for the human story! • Listen to Podcasts
Soccer: • Heading ban in youth soccer • World Cup - Didn't Qualify! (Pay to Play Systems in US.	• I used to love heading the ball in games! • It's a huge part of the game! • I was taught how to do it properly. • How unsafe is it? What's the research? (CTE)	• Soccer Player · Athlete • Coach for young kids • Advocate for kids who can't afford to play on clubs • Injured by concussion when I was 13	• Read more on the research of CTE & soccer • Talk w/ referees on their thoughts • Write a blog on the systems of pay-to-play • Listen to Podcast (ESPNFC)

We began with:

What's in My News?	My Thinking (questions, opinions, ideas, emotions)	My Identity

Now the chart will expand:

What's in My News?	My Thinking (questions, opinions, ideas, emotions)	My Identity	My Ideas for Action

Why Move Beyond Our Initial Thinking?

Identity plays a role in our thinking. Just as we ask kids to look for character changes in stories we read, we want kids to see how their understanding of the world can grow as they grapple with news and different perspectives. Investigating our questions and feelings and taking action will change us. Taking the time to read, listen, talk, and react will yield a more informed citizenry.

When Can We Try This?

- When our students need time to think deeply about an issue they care about.

- When the world hands us a curriculum the night before—that is, anything that is shared publicly on social platforms that we expect will be on kids' minds: attacks, shootings, politics, breaking sports news, parades, rallies, marches, protests, notable deaths shared far and wide.

- When kids want to know more about a topic that is new, important, or that they "heard about" somewhere.

- When there is any measure of crisis at school, as a way to address the issue without artificially smoothing it over. We can take time for the class to pause and slow down, and give support to anyone who urgently needs it.

STEP 1: MODEL YOUR OWN CHART

Gather the kids together, asking them to bring their identity webs and the charts they started in their journals during the previous lesson. Prompt them to look at one piece of their news more deeply and honestly, modeling with an example from your own chart.

OK team, we have all built an individual list of what is in our news at the moment. I am going to take just one piece of my news from my list and think through it a bit more with you. I realized that the Muslim ban makes me really angry and upset inside, but at this point I don't know much more than the headlines I have seen. I have some hard questions to ask, both of myself and of the facts out there.

In order to discuss, comment on, or write about a topic that I care deeply about but may not know a lot about, I must first admit that I have an uninformed opinion. For the ban, I know I have an opinion and that I am angry and hurt, but I want to be able to support how I am feeling with more facts and a broader understanding. I also have to ask some hard questions about why this affects me so much: What in my identity is at stake with this news? If I am ever going to discuss these difficult conversations with someone, especially someone who may see it differently than I do, then I need to be more informed to support why I am feeling the way I am.

At this point, I like to take a quick break from the think-aloud to give the kids a moment to consider why being informed matters.

Turn and tell someone next to you why it is better to be informed than uninformed if you were ever to talk about something you really care or wonder about.

Then, I return to the think-aloud, showing how I use hard questions to consider a topic:

> I already said that I have people in my life that this affects. Including me, potentially. So like I said, I have to start with those hard questions:
>
> > Do I see a part of my identity in this news?
> >
> > Where are the gaps in what I know?
> >
> > Well, as the daughter of Muslim American citizens, I answer yes to that first question. That makes me nervous anytime my relatives fly back and forth to America, their home.
> >
> > There are Muslims all over the world, so why only these countries? Why now?
> >
> > What data indicates that these people are a danger to America?
> >
> > What rights do my family members have should they run into any issues at airports?
> >
> > All right, I asked some questions that may bring up some feelings for me and that is OK. But now I need to figure out a way to get the answers and be more informed.

STEP 2: MODEL

Add the heading for the final column on your chart, *My Ideas for Action*.

> This fourth column is labeled "My Ideas for Action." Can you label your fourth column that as well?

Give kids a minute to label their own chart on the right side of their journal so that the structure now looks like this:

What's in My News?	My Thinking (questions, opinions, ideas, emotions)	My Identity	My Ideas for Action

As kids watch I write down some ways I can take action in the last column as I talk them out. While I am writing I ask them to think alongside me and ask for ideas from them as well.

I know that I can find news articles to read with keywords that will lead me to more news and data sources. I am not just going to write "search the Internet," though, because I have to think specifically about what sources may have information on this, like our Department of Homeland Security, Pew Research Center, or credible news sources (New York Times, Al Jazeera, and the BBC). I need to look at a map to know where these countries are specifically and understand and connect any background knowledge I may have on the region. I may talk to someone who is affected by this ban and look for the human story to this to see how it affects real people.

I can also use writing to take action. I can write to help myself think through my feelings and what I've learned. I can also share my perspective and understandings with others and try to teach or even persuade them.

When I take action to find out more, I will become more informed and my understanding will evolve, even though my feelings may stay the same. I will, I hope, become more knowledgeable about the topic.

STEP 3: GUIDED PRACTICE

Ask students to consider one piece of their news.

OK, look at your list of news and consider the "My Thinking" column you already started. How informed are you? What are you really feeling about the topic? What do you want to know more about? And how can you show your thinking in questions?

Give them a minute to look over what they already have and add to it as they need to. Some of them may have no more space, so providing sticky notes for them to add in any thoughts at this point is a good way to help them extend without feeling confined by the chart's borders.

Then ask them to build an action plan for that piece of news. What will they do to be more informed on the topic?

OK, now contemplate a plan. What action can you take to be a more informed person on this topic?

I have listed things like:

- *Find specific sources to read and research*

- *Interview or talk with someone to get a personal perspective*

- *Study a map*

- *Hunt for the human story*

- *Find someone in the room who can teach you something*

Think about what you can do and write in the column. I challenge you to push beyond just those five action steps. It will look really different for you. And remember to stay away from very general ideas like "Google it." We want to be specific so we are efficient and intentional with our time.

Also think about how you can use writing to take action. How can you use writing to think through what you're feeling and learning? Who needs to hear your perspective? How will you share it with them?

You can either turn and talk with a partner so you have some extra brain power on where to go next, or do some thinking on your own.

Move around the kids as best as you can to see what they are coming up with.

If you started a class newsfeed from the last lesson and want to continue to chart actionable steps for all to see the strategies, this is a good time to do so.

STEP 4: QUICK SHARE OUT

Come back together before you send kids off to try to implement their action plan. Have them share a couple ways they may work to become more evolved in relation to their news. If someone says their next action step is to read, then push them to say what they might read, what specifically they had in mind. If they are short on ideas, consult the group on what else they might try to do.

Do a quick crowd-sourcing step as well to build on your local classroom knowledge and experience:

Let's do one quick go-around the room and just share one thing that is in your news that you would like to become more informed about. As the speaker shares, I want anyone who thinks they can be a resource to that person to give them a silent signal, the shaka sign, that they can see. This way we may find out there are people in the room to talk with or that others share our news as well.

STEP 5: KIDS BEGIN WORK ON THEIR PLANS

Give kids the opportunity to go off and follow their action plan. They may be recording in their journals. They may be annotating with stickies or listening to media. They may be writing to think through their topic or to share their perspective. Rove around the room and support their independent inquiries into their news. Some questions you could ask:

- What is in your news?

- What is your plan to take action?

- How is that going?

- I am looking at your initial thinking on the topic. Has that changed for you? If so, how?

- Have your emotions on the topic changed at all?

- What do you still need to learn about this topic? What will you investigate next?

Students can fill out the fourth column in the chart on their own or as they confer with you. Because the columns are limited by the size of our paper, you and your students may decide to write rough notes elsewhere so they aren't forgotten in the moment and to use the column to bullet-point their thinking.

STEP 6: SHARE AND EXTEND

Bring the group back together to discuss their progress. A few ideas for starting this discussion:

- How did your action plans go?

- Tell someone next to you what action you took today.

- What worked for you and what didn't?

- Did anyone feel uncomfortable or stuck?

- Is anyone ready to share with someone or the whole group how your thinking has evolved?

You might also consider modeling your own evolution of thought, using these stems.

- At first I felt . . . .
- After taking some action, I . . . .
- I became frustrated when . . . .
- Now that I am more informed, I . . . .

↑ FOLLOW-UP

In our social comprehension work, we aim to capture students' passion, anger, and outrage, and support kids in channeling these emotions effectively. When we are clouded by emotions, we do not always see a full picture or range of perspectives. Use this lesson as a touchstone during the year when students find themselves without an informed understanding of something that is important to them. Give students time periodically to return to their plans and learn more about their news. Help students to use the four columns of the chart as necessary to become better informed and to help their thinking to evolve.

↑↓ ADDRESSING TENSIONS

In addition to the tensions listed in the "What's in Your News?" lesson, you might encounter these issues.

1. **Kids are unsure how to source their uninformed opinions.**

   Try this: There are plenty of media literacy lessons that can be built into a lesson like this. Safe searches, keyword searches, locating credible sources, being skeptical and vigilant in an era of 24/7 unvetted reporting, interviewing skills . . . the list goes on. As the lead learner in the room, feel free to map out beforehand what skills to scaffold and adapt according to the needs of your learners.

2. **A range of feelings, including discomfort, may surface as kids continue in this work.**

   Asking students to connect their identity to what they value (their "news") and to explore what they do and don't know puts them in a vulnerable situation. A student may wonder why he is the only one in the class who is concerned about a local civil rights issue. Another student may realize that her news looks far more superficial than other students' lists. Students may be shocked to find that their values clash with those of others in the class, or they may be unpleasantly surprised to find information that contradicts their beliefs.

Try this: Consider where kids can go to take a "brain break"—a place where they can decompress from work that tries their head and heart. My kids and I made a plan that they would walk to the drinking fountain and back. I also play music as they work, if we agree on that as a class. It helps to fill the space and absorbs a lot of the potential energy or frenetic energy in the room.

Synthesis: Making Thinking Visible

Beginning with what is in our news is a way to engage all of our students. It is no secret that human beings learn better when they are interested and engaged in the topic of study. Giving kids the time to pursue the news they care about in their lives leads to meaningful knowledge construction.

The last lesson in this chapter provides an opportunity for wider synthesis. A common thread of the lessons in this book has been to revisit the "At First I Thought . . . Now I Think" pages of their journal, which requires introspection similar to "Evolved Thinking" in the second lesson of this chapter. When returning to students' ongoing journals, you might ask:

- What did you discover about yourself as a learner in these two lessons?
- What do you now know about one of your news items as you've become more informed? What parts of your identity were triggered in these lessons?
- How did you close the gaps between what you didn't know and what you now know?

When we carry news that bears stress, as in the story at the beginning of this chapter, we need to have the tools to respond to it in a way that makes sense to us but doesn't negate the identity of others. It would be very easy after an attack to say, "I feel like all Muslims are terrorists! That's all you hear on the news!" That absolute is grounded in the limited experience he is given by the media. Difficult conversations activate emotions, information, factors of identity, and relational constructs. No wonder most flow with a current of volatility.

Our obligation to kids is to give them opportunities to meet their fears and uninformed opinions with new information, multiple perspectives, and stories of those who might disrupt their assumptions.

5

Finding Humanity in Ourselves and in Others

I once helped treat two severely ill refugee children and educate their father who came straight from the airport as we were the closest hospital, and they could not go any extra minutes without immediate care. They were en route to another city, but both kids had severe kidney failure and needed dialysis often. After an overnight flight, they needed immediate dialysis so they came to us. They created what they could for dialysis in the refugee camp. They [had been] in refugee camps for the past three years. The older one weighed a few pounds more than my toddler, and had broken legs due to such chronic poor nutrition and rickets. The family had multiple kids—all made the trip. I can tell you, it was an incredibly powerful experience. We have never experienced malnourishment in this country like this family. Of all the families I've worked with, nothing compares. But the dad was just like every parent I've ever worked with, just like my husband; his kids playing with My Little Ponies and watching cartoons just like mine do. How can we turn our backs? We shut out innocent good people when we have so much to give, and we perpetuate hate and fear. I pray that the world sees and knows we do not all want this [refugee ban].

—ANNE, NURSE

Because much of the human condition is built around membership, or a belonging to a group, we are constantly responding to difference while coveting sameness. We respond better to those who look like us.

And for those who don't look like us, we can pause and be mindful of when those reactions are based only on partial information or lack of experience, and thus better understand why we act the way we do. The social constructs under which we live can lead us to classify, label with symbols, and eventually dehumanize individuals and groups. Classification, symbolization, and dehumanization are also the early stages in the Ten Stages of Genocide, as defined by the organization Genocide Watch (Stanton 2018). Which is why humanity can quickly slip into atrocities like the Holocaust, the Rwandan genocide, and most recently (though officially undeclared), the Syrian genocide. That may seem grave, but as the lessons of this chapter will examine, if we don't see an individual or group in our universe of obligation or responsibility, we can easily look away as they are pushed further and further out into the margins of society, where they are no longer viewed as human.

The Ten Stages of Genocide.

By Dr. Gregory H. Stanton, Founding Chairman, Genocide Watch

1. **Classification**–dividing society into "us" vs. "them," stripping citizenship of targeted groups;

2. **Symbolization**–naming or imposing symbols on classifications (Jews, Tutsi, stars);

3. **Discrimination**–using legal or cultural power to exclude groups from full civil rights;

4. **Dehumanization**–portraying targeted groups as subhuman vermin, cockroaches, diseases, traitors, infidels, criminals, or terrorists;

5. **Organization**–organizing, training, and arming hate groups, armies, and militias;

6. **Polarization**–arresting moderate opponents as traitors, propaganda against "enemies of the people;"

7. **Preparation**–planning, identification of victims, training and arming killers;

8. **Persecution**–expropriation, forced displacement to ghettos, concentration camps;

9. **Extermination**–physical killing, torture, mass rape, social and cultural destruction;

10. **Denial**–minimizing statistics, blaming victims or war or famine, denying "intent."

Discussions of genocide might feel distant from the situations we encounter first-hand in our own lives on a typical day. However, the dispositions that are foundational to atrocities are at work in our lives every day. We react to the small and large tragedies that blast our newsfeeds with great shock and horror: *How did we get here?* The choices we make each day are a form of voting. Where we send our kids to school, where we shop, where we buy our homes and the areas we avoid. Sadly, it isn't difficult to see various traits that make up the stages of genocide in news events, structural systems, and even state-sanctioned policies. Genocide is not hypothetical. History reminds us that it begins with the small bias-filled, insidious choices and commentary people make every single day, banked over time.

In the long arc of our country's history there has always been classification, there has always been the "othering" of some group. What can we do about it?

We fight these destructive forces by finding and examining our humanity first. That is, get in touch with the elements that make us (socialized) human beings—the ability to learn, love, observe, empathize, feel pain, and inflict pain. We can be ever-mindful not to fall into the trap of *only* acknowledging our "shared humanity" or the notion that "we are all the same." Yes, we all belong to the human race, but there are so many different layers to our identities that we are all unique. We can't let ourselves fall into the trap of erasure. Don't erase a person's identity to make yourself more comfortable. Color blindness ("I don't see color! We are all human beings!") or blind spot bias ("You may have bias, but I don't; I see everyone

The social constructs under which we live can lead us to classify, label with symbols, and eventually dehumanize individuals and groups.

FINDING HUMANITY IN OURSELVES AND IN OTHERS

as an equal") are dangerous lenses that can lull us into thinking if we ignore tension it will go away. We need to see the whole of who people are. That can mean pausing to consider how skin color, gender, or ability has an impact on their experiences in society.

While we are working to build kids' capacity for empathy, we can honor how they see the world. *Empathy* is a banner term lately. We see it everywhere. In mission and vision statements, in speeches, headlining book lists, and on education websites. We want kids to "have empathy" or "activate empathy" when presented with a moving story, image, or headline as if it is a gadget that switches on when we push a button. We want them to "put themselves in someone else's shoes."

> *Imagine being Anne Frank hidden away in the attic during the Holocaust.*
> *How do you think Rosa Parks felt sitting down on that bus?*
> *If you were in [insert anyone]'s situation, how would you feel?*

And then we might even assess whether their empathy was correct or not. This might be with a strike of a pen on a rubric or with a horrified response to their attempt at comprehension. We make those teachable empathy moments more about us and barely hear how kids are responding with the compassion and curiosity they already have.

We have the ability to humanize the headlines.

Picture this: The first time my young niece saw a group of women in full niqab, the Muslim veil for the face that leaves only the eyes visible, she said, "Mama, look! Who are those people? Ninjas? Why are the ninjas out during the day?"

Perhaps you've seen a child make an observation like this—an attempt to connect what she is seeing with what she thinks she already knows—followed by a swift and icy response from a parent or adult who has judged the child's empathy to be lacking, or who is embarrassed by the comment being made in public. My sister had a developmentally appropriate response to my niece's attempt to comprehend: she explained the niqab to her, and didn't shut her down or try to ignore her confusion. This is a model we can all emulate in our own lives, regardless of our own personal discomfort. And if we don't know answers to our children's questions, we can create opportunities to learn together.

Kids bring an incredible sense of empathy and justice to this world. They understand fairness at an early age, and are often the members of our society who feel and show an organic wonder and compassion for others (sometimes even before they are speaking or conventionally literate). Let's consider how their experiences shape how (or if) they "feel" for others. Let's not edit their responses to fit our idea of empathy, losing sight of who they are and how they make meaning of their world.

The lessons in this chapter are a culmination of the lessons throughout the book that have asked kids to hold up both a mirror and a magnifying glass to their identity. They draw from many lessons earlier in this book that ask students to activate identity, call for candor, and reveal bias. When we ask ourselves honest questions about how we may see our own humanity in others, we will be far more adept at being compassionate citizens.

You have to be able to see the humanity in others before you can activate your empathy by self-identifying and making connections. Anne, in the opening anecdote, was able to see her kids in the children of the refugee family. She drew comparisons between her husband and the father of the young patient—both showed unconditional love for their children. She recognized the humanity in this family from another world away through a lens of self-identifying: "his kids playing with My Little Ponies and watching cartoons just like mine do" and "he was a parent like any parent I work with." She was able to shift to compassion toward refugees whom she can see as "innocent good people." We might think that Anne, whose career is focused on helping others, looks to find the good in everyone. But this is not a genetic predisposition toward compassion; it is an evolved piece of her character. As you consider the lesson titled "Our Universe of Obligation," you will see how people begin to matter to others, not because of a job description or a formal responsibility, but because we reconsider how we process, respond to, and reflect on our connections when we are confronted with the stories of others. This is when we, like Anne, can see that humans are not a situation, issue, or headline; they are members of a family, just like our own. We have the ability to humanize the headlines.

Broadening Our Ideas About Who We Are Responsible To and For

Our Universe of Obligation

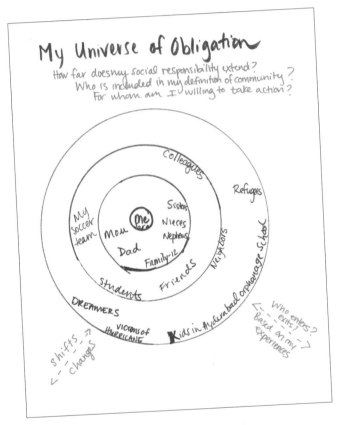

What Is My Universe of Obligation?

The *universe of obligation* is what sociologist Helen Fein defines as people "toward whom obligations are owed, to whom rules apply, and whose injuries call for [amends]" (quoted in Strom 1994, 56).

This lesson is adapted from the organization Facing History and Ourselves. It asks students to consider the people or groups toward whom they feel a responsibility or obligation. I am using the terms interchangeably here because responsibility is a common term used in schools around citizenship. Feel free to use either *obligation* or *responsibility* in your classroom.

Why Consider One's Universe of Obligation?

The painstaking norms of sitting in lunchrooms, playing outside at recess, supporting teammates on school teams, working in groups in class, bullying in the halls, hazing in locker rooms, teasing on the bus, and even the simple act of smiling and saying hello all rest on an individual's perception of whether or not other people are part of their universe of obligation. Kids make many decisions day to day on whether or not to act on behalf of someone else, on where someone falls in their universe of obligation. In this activity we are making that thinking visible so we can "see" who we feel responsible for, then notice and question how and why our universe of obligation may shift in life.

When Do We Use Our Universe of Obligation?

- When we want students to consider their own circles of trust, actions, and biases. (This does not need to wait until late in the year.)
- When we want to better understand the choices people or characters have made.
- When we read stories of "upstanders," people who decide to help or to stand up, no matter the consequence. Conversely, when we read stories of bystanders, or people who looked on, knowingly choosing not to help.
- When we read about times in history when an individual or a group of people had the choice to act, and about the implications of that choice.

STEP 1: ASK STUDENTS TO RECALL BEING AN UPSTANDER

Bring kids to the meeting area with their journals. Prime this activity with some silent visualizing and remembering:

> *Let's take a quiet minute as we get settled for the lesson. You may want to look down or close your eyes to help you focus and visualize.*
>
> *Think about a time when you were an upstander or when you helped someone. Someone in need. Maybe it was just a little thing; maybe it was a big thing. You won't be sharing this; this memory is just for you.*

Upstander is a term I use so frequently with my students that they'll know it by now, but if it's new to your students, you can explain it this way: Upstanders are "active and informed human beings who will make thoughtful and brave choices in their own lives, in their communities, and [in the] world" (Daniels and Ahmed 2014, 4). Upstanders do the right thing by others, even when it is not the easy thing.

As kids think, you can guide their visualization with these questions, slowly offering them more to unpack.

Maybe it was a family member, a brother or sister.

Or a friend in the neighborhood.

Or a classmate at school.

Maybe it was a stranger.

What did that person need?

How did you know that?

What did you do?

How was it received?

What did it take for you to help them?

What did it feel like for you and for them?

Maybe you are seeing a time when someone helped you, and that is OK, too.

Then, signal to the kids to bring their attention back to the room, and ask them to write about this experience.

OK, thanks for taking the time to do that. In your journals on a fresh page, go ahead and write a little bit about what you just visualized and thought about.

Give students one or two minutes to write. If they're on fire to write more, let them go a few more minutes. Then bring them back, but no need to share out. They will revisit what they've written later in the lesson.

STEP 2: INTRODUCE YOUR UNIVERSE OF OBLIGATION

Show students the graphic tool they'll be using for this lesson, titled "My Universe of Obligation." You may choose to have a sheet ready to include in their journals with the graphic already drawn, or you may have them draw the circles themselves.

I have drawn four concentric circles here. Can you do the same and label them on the inside, 1–4, just like I have. Make sure they are big enough to write inside.

Some of you have already noticed the title of this chart, "My Universe of Obligation." It is a big concept to consider so I am going to show you what I mean.

Today we are going to be thinking about people or groups whom we feel responsibility for, or an obligation toward. These concentric circles with you in the middle stand for the people or groups that surround your universe. You are at the center of your decisions and choices; who you feel responsible toward is part of that. Each circle after your own (which is number 1) represents the people to whom you feel most obligated. As the circles go out, the people don't become less important. You consider them important just by including them at all.

Turn and talk with someone next to you for thirty seconds about what the word obligation might mean to you. You can talk about any part of the word you are familiar with or you can even go for the whole title, "My Universe of Obligation." It sounds like something out of a superhero comic, doesn't it? "MY UNIVERSE OF OBLIGATION!"

Listen in as kids are talking. If you hear anything that you feel may help others, chart it somewhere with the student's or pair's names next to it as they chat. Bring them back together and either share what you wrote or have them discuss a few ideas they came up with.

Bring them back to the graphic tool. I like to show them how I complete the entire chart and then let them do their own, but you might choose to alternate between having students watch you model one circle and trying it for themselves. As long as students understand what each level means, either method works.

Here's how I model completing the entire chart:

OK, so watch me. The first step in filling this out is easy. I am going to write my name inside the innermost circle, which I'll call circle number 1. This puts me at the center of my universe looking out. Think of it as a physical location, not an indication that I am selfish and that everything revolves around me.

Go ahead and write your name in your circle number 1.

In the next circle, circle 2, I am going to write the people to whom I feel the greatest obligation. These are the people I would without question be an upstander for, no matter what.

Continue modeling, emphasizing that students don't need to name particular individuals on their charts (particularly classmates!).

The people I am willing to take a risk for, even put myself in danger for, no matter the consequence, are my family. There are many of them, so I am just going to write family. Later I may add parents, sisters, cousins, nephews, nieces, aunts, and uncles. That is what I mean by family. Your circle may look very different from mine. As you complete your own charts, don't worry about using individuals' names.

So, I am also going to write "friends," but I am thinking of who those specific friends are as I write this. I'm not going to weigh whether each friend belongs in circle 2, circle 3, or circle 4. In fact, I can even write friends in all of the circles, knowing that I am closer to some friends than others, but that all of them are within my universe of obligation.

You may already have begun thinking about whom you are going to write in circle 2. That's great! In circle 3, I am still going to think about whom I feel responsible for after that group of people in circle 2. These people are still really important, but my obligation to them is not as great as to my family. My friends back home in Chicago are going to be in this circle. They are always there for me. I'll write Chicago friends but not all of their names. I may add a couple more names to this circle as I think things through.

The next level, circle 4, is the same idea. I have an obligation to these people but not as great as in circle 2 or 3. The school where I am currently located and the teachers and kids in this circle are groups of people that I am obligated to and I feel a responsibility for day to day. Of course, all of the people who are in your diagram are important to you, no matter what circle they are in. You're simply using the circles to help you consider all of the people who are important to you, beyond those in your innermost circle. We will talk more about how things can shift between the circles.

STEP 3: MAP UNIVERSES OF OBLIGATION

Kids typically get the idea at this stage, and some of them may already be writing their own. Give them time to work.

Can you try this now while we are all here together? Some of you may have already started. This shouldn't take long, but be thoughtful. Something important to remember is that this is entitled "MY Universe of Obligation" because it is mine. YOUR universe of obligation is yours, not what anyone else thinks it should be or what you think I am going to think is right or wrong. Your universe of obligation chart is something we may use over and over again as we study other people and communities who have had to make choices about who was in their universe of obligation.

As kids are working you may notice that some finish at different times or use yours as a model for their own and are done. Take a minute to confer with them if you notice this happening.

When the class seems ready to move on, bring them back together and thank them for their thoughtful work.

STEP 4: RECONSIDER WHO'S IN YOUR UNIVERSE OF OBLIGATION

Give the kids an opportunity to connect their own experience as upstanders with the chart they've created.

You did some remembering and writing when we first started this lesson. I asked you to think about a time when you helped someone or someone helped you. Now, looking back, you may have connected the dots and thought about that story with a responsibility or obligation lens.

Is that person whom you helped in your universe of obligation? Do you feel like you have to change or add anything if they are not? Do you think you were in theirs?

Turn and talk about that with someone for a minute.

Because you told students at the start that they won't have to share their story, you can remind them here that the question is really whether that person is in their universe of obligation and vice versa, and if they're now thinking of changing or adding anything in their universe of obligation as a result. That is all they really need to share, though you may have students who choose to share more.

After a few minutes, bring the class back together and introduce the idea of changes in one's universe of obligation.

> *If you were the person being helped, you may not know the answer to the question about whether or not you are in their universe of obligation, because you aren't that person. And if you were the person doing the helping, you may not see that person in the universe of obligation you crafted today. That is OK. Let me share with you why that happens.*
>
> *Sometimes we are faced with situations where an individual or group of individuals comes into our universe of obligation. We may not initially view them as someone we feel an obligation toward, but then something changes: perhaps we get to know them more, they become closer to us, we listen to and understand their story more, or something happens in the moment like an accident or emergency. Here's an example: during Hurricane Katrina, my friend went down to help the victims.*

I physically slide my finger from the outside of the circles all the way to circle 2 to demonstrate this as I talk.

> *The people of New Orleans may not even have been in any of her circles, but when she became more informed as to what happened down there, the victims moved into her number 2 circle: she felt very responsible for them. She felt an obligation tugging at her as someone who could go down and help.*
>
> *We are going to read a story where this happens—where a character's universe of obligation shifts due to a new interaction they have with someone whom they never before met.*

STEP 5: SEE A UNIVERSE SHIFT

Next you'll give kids time to read a story and track a shift in a character's universe of obligation. For this lesson, I often ask kids to read "Thank You, Ma'am" by Langston Hughes, a classic story that can be used for a myriad of lessons. If students are familiar with it already, using it again targets the focus of this lesson even more. There is much value in rereading.

Ask the students to consider a particular character's universe of obligation as they read.

I am going to send you back to read one of my favorite short stories. It's called "Thank You, Ma'am," and it's by Langston Hughes. I want you to consider the universe of obligation of either of the characters in this story and whether you see their universe shift. I will tell you that they are strangers to each other in the beginning of the story.

> *When you are finished reading the story, make some tracks of your thinking in your journal. Consider what we know about the universe of obligation for these two characters. What changed for them and why? I will be around to support you.*

Here, I don't ask kids for a specific product or a completed chart. I keep the task from being rigid because I want them to experience the piece with what we are discussing in mind. I observe them to see if they need more guidance, and then confer with them to support them.

STEP 6: CONSIDER WHAT YOUR UNIVERSE OF OBLIGATION SAYS ABOUT YOU

Help students to consider the patterns they see in their own universes of responsibility. I might begin this conversation by saying:

> *Take a moment to privately take stock of who is in your circles. People who look like you? People with the same hobbies, interests, or backgrounds? Other able-bodied individuals?*

The exercise of identifying those we feel a sense of responsibility for is similar to another antibias exercise: identifying whom we trust. What is uncovered in both of these approaches is that our list of trusted individuals tends to look like us unless we are actively living a life where we are proximate to people and experiences outside our own identity circles. Both exercises reveal how our individual identity and our group membership will lead us to act with bias in life. You can reveal this insight to students without making them feel bad about their own circles by phrasing this in terms of someone else's experience. For example, I might say:

> *Remember my friend who went down to New Orleans? Well, at first, she had no one in her circles who didn't look like her. Her family, the people in her church, her friends—they all look like her and share similar perspectives. Those are the people she trusts, loves, and feels a responsibility for. When she went to New Orleans, she told me that she realized she was in an all-black neighborhood the whole time she was there, and that she had never spent time with even one black person at*

home. She learned a lot that week and realized how limited her view was on an entire group of individuals whom she didn't know how to trust, solely based on images and messages she had in her mind from media and society.

STEP 7: SHARE/DISCUSSION

To help students process these concepts, allow time for them to discuss:

- what it means to have a universe of obligation
- how we decide who we have in ours
- when we make shifts in our universe of obligation based on our experiences

Revisit the story you chose to read and discuss and interpret how, when, and why the universe of obligation may have shifted for the character(s). Structure the discussion in the style that works best for your learning community. Here's a "discussion menu" of options that have helped my students to share ideas over the years:

Discussion Menu

Table talks: Small groups at tables

Campfire: Whole group in a circle

Online forum: Discussion using a tech tool such as Edmodo, Padlet, Voice Thread, Google Classroom

Written conversation: Pairs or small groups discuss through writing and responding to short, timed letters to one another (Daniels and Daniels 2013).

Discussion party: Pairs discuss, then merge to form groups of four, then merge again to form groups of eight.

Listen in on the conversations. If discussions seem to be focused more on the events of the story than on universes of responsibility, gently redirect students.

↑ FOLLOW-UP

In real life, our sense of obligation affects the decisions we make every day when we encounter "othering," teasing, bullying, and, more prevalent today, hate crimes. How we define who we are responsible for, outside of our family and friends, can be guided by what we are familiar with and who we look like. However, if we actively work to get proximate to other people, our sense of obligation becomes much wider and more inclusive. We see people not as "others" but as human beings.

Revisit the concept of the universe of obligation or ask students to reflect on and consider updating their own whenever you want to help kids to:

- understand and prevent "othering."

- make sense of decisions (unconscious and conscious) to be bystanders or upstanders, whether these decisions are in their own lives, in texts, or in current events.

- trace how bias (in this case, the bias toward those people who are in our universe of obligation and against those who are not) affects decisions and actions.

- consider who their universe of obligation does not include, why, and how they might broaden their universe.

⇅ ADDRESSING TENSIONS

1. **Kids feel like they have to include every single friend because their chart is "public."**

   Try this: Take this out of the equation early by telling them that this is not a popularity or friendship contest but a genuine way in which they see the world. They can be inclusive by simply writing "friends." They can also consider the friends who have been there for them, to whom they would like to return the obligation. We want to shift away from kids' desire to include all their friends, pets, and so on, and focus them more on what makes someone a part of their universe of obligation. How do you determine who is in it? How might a complete stranger move into it?

Suggested Resource Stack for Universe of Obligation

Picture Books:

Each Kindness by Jacqueline Woodson

The Invisible Boy by Tracy Ludwig

Essay:

"Little Things Are Big" by Jesús Colón

Novels:

Seedfolks by Paul Fleischman

Any Small Goodness: A Novel of the Barrio by Tony Johnston

Long-Form Nonfiction:

The Sunflower by Simon Wiesenthal

Short Stories:

"The Lottery" by Shirley Jackson

"Thank You, Ma'am" by Langston Hughes

"The Scholarship Jacket" by Marta Salinas

"The Wrong Lunch Line" by Nicholasa Mohr

Videos:

"Not in Our Town: Billings Montana" (story and video), niot.org

"The Bystander" by Osnat Epstein

Social Media:

Hashtags on social media sometimes lead me to stories of
upstanders who brought strangers into their universe of obligation.
I am, of course, careful and critical in my search of these.

Understanding Others' Perspectives

Intent Versus Impact

What is the Difference between Intent Versus Impact?

In all forms of communication there is a sender and a receiver. We send messages with a spectrum of intent: to inform, to congratulate, to compliment, to show gratitude, and sometimes to disrupt, hurt, or degrade. Being fully aware of the intention behind our messages and signals is only part of the equation of communication. There is also the impact that message has on the receiver. Because people receive information through filters of their own identity and experiences, the message received can be very different from the one intended.

Why Teach Intent Versus Impact?

The messages all people send, whether verbally, digitally, or nonverbally, go through a series of filters on the receiving end.

Consider times you have heard a student agonize over what a peer meant in a communication, such as including a heart emoji in a comment on social media. (*Why did he send it? Does he mean it? Does he like me? Should I send one back? What would that mean?*) Or consider situations when you have been dumbfounded by a response to something you've said or done. Perhaps, for example, you think you've given someone a compliment, only to see that they're angry or hurt as a result.

When the impact of a communication is very different from its intent, people who sent the message may try to defend themselves by saying, "That's not what I meant!" However, that excuse doesn't mend the damage done. Moreover, it implies that the perspective of the person who sent the message is the only perspective that matters. The work of social comprehension requires us to be mindful not only of what we mean to say, but how we say it, and how the messages we send (intentional or not) impact others.

When Do We Teach Intent Versus Impact?

- At the beginning of the year when we are building partner, small-group, and whole-group discussion skills. Then revisit as necessary throughout the year.
- Before students begin commenting digitally on each other's work or social media posts.

STEP 1: SEE, THINK, AND WONDER WITH AN IMAGE

Begin with a blank three-column chart to track students' responses. Label the columns "See," "Think," and "Wonder."

Show students a sports team logo that depicts a Native American. When I've taught this lesson, I've found strong resources that focus on the Cleveland Indians. You may find even more resources about this team moving forward as a result of the team's 2018 announcement that they will retire their Chief Wahoo logo. There are also many other teams that could be a focus for this lesson, such as the Washington Redskins or the Atlanta Braves.

> *I want you to take a look at this image of the Cleveland Indians logo.*
> *When you look at this picture, what do you see? Let's try and make a list,*
> *so think specifically, such as "I see eyes."*

Let some volunteers share and write their comments in the first column. When I've used this lesson, students have mentioned a feather, red skin, teeth, or a smile.

Next, ask kids to consider what the logo represents. They need to think deeper here by using their observations to draw an inference. Let kids turn and talk on this one. Listen in to their talks and encourage them to build off of what they noticed about the image.

> *Using what you saw in this list, try to think with a partner about this*
> *image. What do you notice and what does it make you think about? There*
> *is no wrong answer.*

Write the comments in the second column. You may get responses like those I've heard in my classrooms:

- I think it is a Native American or Indian.
- I think that it is cartoonish.
- I think he is happy.

Finally, ask students what they wonder about this logo.

Building off of what you see and think, what questions do you have about this logo? For example, "I wonder why . . ." or "I wonder if . . ." Turn and talk with a partner to share your questions.

Again, let them talk and build together. Listen in and add some of the questions you hear to the third column of your chart.

STEP 2: INTRODUCE INTENT

Draw a T-chart with the left side labeled *intent* and the right side labeled *impact*.

The Cleveland Indians are a baseball team in Ohio. This is their mascot. What are mascots? Why do teams have mascots? What do they mean for the team?

Can you please write about that in your notebooks for just a minute?

You'll likely get a variety of responses when students share out or when you read over shoulders as kids write in their notebooks. Chart these on the left side of the T-chart with the student's name. Here are a few responses I've heard:

- Mascots can be animals or people.
- Teams choose powerful mascots to represent them.
- Mascots are something that teams and fans like.
- Mascots are symbols.
- Maybe they honor the group or animal.
- Everyone can wear the colors and mascot to show their pride.
- Teams think that mascots bring them luck.

While you are charting some of the answers, introduce the word *intent* in context.

I am going to take some of your thoughts up here while I introduce the word intent. Your intent is what you mean by your actions. I am wondering: What was the intent of the Cleveland Indians when they chose this mascot?

Let's look at the ideas you're mentioning, and try applying them to this situation. Here are a couple of examples:

- The intention of having this Indian as a mascot is to bring the team luck.
- Their intent in using the Indian is that Indians are powerful and so are they.

Is that making sense? Does anyone want to take a risk and try to use the word intent or intentions with the ideas up here?

STEP 3: LISTEN TO HOW A MESSAGE WAS RECEIVED

Now that kids have had the chance to make some inferences and read the image for what it projects to them, you can introduce the word *impact*.

> *We've talked about the intentions a team might have in using a logo of a person to represent them. They may have the best of intentions in honoring brave warriors, to take a few words from you. But in all forms of communication, even images, it goes both ways. There is the intention of your message you are sending. And then there is the impact it has on someone else or a community of people—how they receive that message. Now we're going to take a look at the impact, or effect, that the Cleveland Indians mascot has had on other people.*

Share a video or text in which those who oppose the use of a Native American as a mascot give their perspectives on the symbol. Look for sources in which those who are protesting the symbol give their reasons for doing so as well as sources that focus on the mascot's supporters.

A helpful resource for this lesson is a video from the *New York Times,* "They Think We're Just Historical" (you can find it at www.nytimes.com /interactive/2016/12/09/us/confronting-racist-objects.html?_r=0).

The following texts could also be used for this lesson:

- "Insult or Honor?" by Alessandra Potenza, *Scholastic News*, August 29, 2014
- "American High Schools Cling to 'Redskins' Nickname" by Zac Boyer, *Washington Times*, June 1, 2014
- "Insults, Not Honor: A Message from the American Indian Movement," Cleveland American Indian Movement, April 2007
- "Cleveland Indians Will Abandon Chief Wahoo Logo Next Year" by David Waldstein, *New York Times*, January 29, 2018.

As kids watch or read, don't require them to take notes. Instead, ask them to watch, listen, or read intently. Let them focus on the message's impact. I teach my kids to just give a silent signal in the air if they need time to process or if they want to write, and I will pause for them.

Once they've seen or read the source, have students turn and talk.

> *Turn to someone next to you to discuss this source. What have you learned about the impact Chief Wahoo has had on people?*

As kids are talking, try to fill out the right side of the chart as you listen in. It may help other pairs as they talk to see the ideas written down. Continue to write names with corresponding ideas. When the kids have had enough time to talk through their ideas, bring them back together and offer them an opportunity to see the source again. If the source also includes comments from people who support the use of the logo, you can use a second pass through the source to add ideas to the intent side of the chart. The fans may say things like, "It has always been this way!" (*tradition*) or "We are honoring them!" (*honor*).

> *OK, I eavesdropped a bit and lots of you did some awesome listening and really heard the impact Chief Wahoo has on many people. I wrote a few things down that I heard you say about how it impacts people to see Chief Wahoo on the Indians' uniforms or people dressed up like cartoonish Indians. We can look at the source one more time, if you'd like.*

If the kids want to see the source again, show it.

STEP 4: RESEARCH

We want students always to see the perspectives of both sides of a difficult conversation. If they already feel strongly about one side or the other, we can help them first seek to understand before their need to be understood. The purpose of the intent versus impact T-chart is to help kids to see both sides and then allow them to muddle through how they may feel after studying both perspectives.

> *OK, we have been able to look at the logo of Chief Wahoo of the Cleveland Indians and list some ideas about what the intent of the team may be. We have also heard about the impact of that logo. Some questions have come up during your See, Think, Wonder exercise and also through the partner chats you've had. I want to give you time to research the history and maybe some of the controversy over Chief Wahoo with the Cleveland Indians.*

Giving kids time to research on their own shows that we value their independence in finding answers to tough topics and will support them through their thinking, rather than allowing our bias to completely sway their inquiry.

If students are using devices to research, pull from their T-chart and the discussion to share some useful search terms. Another option is to bookmark sites for them in a shared location.

If students are using printed articles, you can use those same keyword searches to find appropriate text for your readers. Resources like Newsela, *Sports Illustrated*,

Vox, *Scholastic News*, and *New York Times Upfront* all have articles on this topic. It has been widely debated for decades.

Send students off for about ten minutes to gather quotes and evidence. Because this is a short amount of research time, we don't want to bog them down with carefully made templates and planners to fill in. Instead, to keep motivation high, they can add to the T-chart you've made together using sticky notes, or write questions or curiosities in their journals. What you may find is a lot of visible and audible thinking (the sounds of social comprehension at work): "Whoa, look at this!" and "Did you know this, Ms. Ahmed!?" I am totally OK with this talk. Learning is social, and difficult conversations come with lots of reaction and emotion.

As the kids work, crowd source the room to what resources they're using. As time permits, list those sources so that there is a communal bank if they need to be referenced again.

STEP 5: WRITE A CONVERSATION

Coming back together, students have now explored the following during their inquiry into this relevant topic: an image, a source, partner talks, whole-group talks, the perspective of others in their class, and the many voices found during their research time.

Now they are ready to discuss their own views through some independent sustained writing.

> *I have made a list up here of all the places where you drew in new knowledge around this issue of the Cleveland Indians mascot—for many teams, in fact. Wow! We are so much more informed than we were at the beginning of this inquiry.*
>
> *We are going to spend some time writing how we feel about all this, taking into account the intent of teams using certain mascots and the impact this has had on people and communities. I am going to ask you to consider how you feel about it and transfer all those thoughts and feelings and knowledge through a letter to a partner, a pen pal! I am looking specifically for writers who can include the words* impact *and* intent *in their explanations. Consider that your challenge!*

Assign partners or have students choose someone they will write to during this activity. An alternative to pairing at random can be to pair kids who have differing opinions or are on the fence about how they feel. This may produce some challenging conversations.

Project these directions for the students:

1. Each person in the partnership will have a sheet of paper.

2. Address the partner in a salutation (*Hi!* or *Dear* _____, or *Wassup!*) at the top of the page.

3. Put the date in the upper-right-hand corner.

4. You will have two minutes to write to your partner about how you are feeling or about one of our discussion questions that we came up with together. Both of you write at the same time.

5. At the end of the two minutes you will hear a signal telling you to stop and finish your thought.

6. A few seconds later, you will hear me say "switch!" Trade letters with your partner at this point.

7. You'll have about thirty seconds to read your partner's letter.

8. At the end of the thirty seconds you will hear another signal that prompts you to begin writing them back. You will have two minutes.

9. At the end of the two minutes, you will pass your paper back to your partner and thank them for the time they spent with you.

The most important things to consider here are your partner's thoughts and opinions. Remember, in difficult conversations, we want to listen to understand, not just listen to respond. You and your partner may not agree. The best thing that can happen is that you learn a new way of looking at something that you didn't consider before.

To help get kids started, you can frame some of the students' comments from earlier in the lesson as questions they might consider. This really empowers the kids whose question you use. For example, when I've taught this lesson, I've drawn the following questions from comments the kids had made in earlier parts of the lesson:

- How does the intent to use the Cleveland Indians mascot, Chief Wahoo, impact many people?

- Is it an insult or an honor to have a mascot represent a group of people?

- Where do you stand on the issue of mascots that represent Native Americans and why?

- If we are aware that people are offended by the use of mascots and logos representing their community, how do we move forward?

These are student-generated from classes I have worked with, so while I think they are pretty great, it is always best to see where your students can go with their dialogue and generate their own questions for discussion.

As students are writing vigorously to their partners, it's up to you to keep to the timeline outlined above. While the kids are writing, you can walk around and support anyone who isn't self-starting or read over a few shoulders. Try not to invite conversations as you don't want to deter from the writing focus. Because the work is timed, the kids write fast and furiously, often shaking their tired hands in triumph at the end.

If written conversations are new to your students, they may be eager to talk about the experience of writing to each other. If so, give them an opportunity to share what the process felt like, what they can celebrate about their partners and their communication, and whether/how the conversation affected their thinking on the topic.

STEP 6: SHARE

Our goal in this work is not for students to become experts on this one issue but for them to consider the wider implications of intention and impact, listen to and understand the perspectives of all sides, and be aware of the impact of their own intentions in their everyday lives. If this broader view has not yet come up in conversation, guide students toward it now.

It might be tempting simply to tell the kids that intent and impact can vary widely, that individuals' identities affect both intent and impact, and that social comprehension requires us to consider not just our own intent but also the impact of our words and actions on others. However, students are more likely to take these ideas to heart if they work through them on their own. To support this, you might open a discussion around these four points:

1. How does a person's identity affect his or her ability to see how his or her intentions impact others?
2. How does a person's identity affect how he or she is impacted by others' actions?
3. What have you learned about the power of intent versus the power of impact?
4. What are some ways you might reconsider the impact of your intentions in your everyday life?

↑ FOLLOW-UP

The practice of being aware of *intent* and *impact* is a powerful tool. It names a problem that can be so deeply embedded in individuals' perspectives that it can seem unsolvable—that seemingly uncrossable gulf between ideas, when people can't seem to find common ground. Our hope is that kids start to understand that the messages we send can have a different impact than we intend due to the many filters we all have acquired as human beings. Our messages have impact.

You can remind students about this lesson to help them understand the forces at work when intent and impact are not the same, either in their own lives, or in the stories and history you study together as a class. This lesson will also give you a handle on how to address issues in which you hear people say:

- That's not what I meant!
- Don't take this the wrong way, but . . . .
- I'm not a racist, but . . . .
- You should feel (honored, proud, happy) . . . .

Being aware of the gap between intent and impact can help the person who is sending the message both to reframe the message and reconsider whether they've made an effort to truly understand the receiver's viewpoint.

⇅ ADDRESSING TENSIONS

1. **Students do not truly consider another perspective or perhaps have deeply rooted beliefs from home, which causes verbal conflict.**

    Everyone is entitled to their opinion in a classroom that works through difficult conversations and toward social comprehension. Again, this is not about our teacher bias and getting kids to where we think they should be on a specific side of a topic. If there is any discomfort during this lesson, it is important to notice it and make some decisions on how to move forward. The goal is not to get all the kids in your classroom to protest the Cleveland Indians.

    Try this: If you have to stop the class in moments that get heated or emotional, this is an important time to acknowledge established discussion norms of the class, especially about how to agree to disagree and move forward.

    Before the lesson or before the letter writing, remind the community of the anchor charts you created as a class (see Chapter 2) for strategies they can use when they disagree or when they need to get into the listening zone to understand someone. You might even ask the class or individuals to pinpoint two strategies they will employ from the chart should they need to do so in the heat of the moment. This way they will be proactive with the tools they have rather than reactive in a difficult conversation.

Synthesis: Making Thinking Visible

The lessons in this chapter teach us that in dealing with the most challenging conversations, we will learn more as well as strengthen our relationships with others if we maintain both an understanding of who we are and a little humility. Then we use that self-awareness and humility to see the humanity in others.

In their ongoing journals, students have been using the "At First I Thought . . . Now I Think" prompts to reflect on their growth. Continuing that work after the lessons in this chapter recenters us as learners.

When our eyes are open to the world around us, when we let others into our universe of obligation, we are less likely to fall into the traps of perpetuated fear and hate. We don't see refugees as a drain or a threat, but as people: a father who wishes for his daughter to have the universal right to live, as any parent would. We want kids to comprehend a little more each day how the choices they make, the language they use, and the way they think matter—consciously and subconsciously.

In the spirit of finding humanity, the focus of this chapter, it's important to take a moment to consider how we are responding to what students write in these "At First I Thought . . . Now I Think" journals. These journals are not "gotchas" or documents validating our teaching. If we can't fathom why a student doesn't shift on an issue, we must remember that this is *their* journal, not ours. Our students are kids. They are working hard to grasp ideologies and concepts many adults still struggle with. If these journals are really a place for their thinking, we must respect that thinking. For example, we might respond to something we disagree with by asking questions rather than attempting to correct.

You can also use this point in your progress through these lessons to help students self-explore and reflect on earlier entries. You might ask them to choose their favorite entry, or a line or two from an entry that will stay with them or that shows change, and invite them to share these lines either anonymously or publicly. For example, students can read them, graffiti them on a shared space, use them as a starting point for a longer piece, or even build a digital showcase of their thinking.

6

Facing Crisis Together

Hurt

Pain

Anger

Ambivalence

Frustration

Sadness

Concern

Hate

Illness

Fear

Exhaustion

Nervousness

Helplessness

Emptiness

Contempt

Wonder

Aloofness

Aggression

Validation

Love

When we face a crisis individually, there is inevitably an undulating pattern of emotions. Where our response may begin, swing, hang, or end in time depends on how we self-identify, how we see others, and our universe of obligation, not entirely on the event itself. To test that premise, take the last event or tragedy you can think of and consider how you responded, then how someone else you know responded. Did emotions run in lockstep, or were they wildly different? Has that drawn a figurative wedge between you and people you've held close your whole life?

Why do you think that is? Consider your own identity and then how that other person self-identifies.

When we look tragedy in the eye, together, we can assume that every single human being around us is feeling a different emotion, at a different pace, at a different point in time, and to a different degree than we are. My live, on-the-spot, visual analogy as I key this sentence to page is the traffic in Bangkok I'm currently watching through my window. At any given time, there are six (deliberate) lanes of traffic moving in a somewhat organized common direction, but there is speeding, pausing, inching, walking, riding, U-turning, weaving, halting, stalling, and coasting. Rarely are any two objects the same on this road, nor are they in unison. Time and space continue to move, but how do we make sense of it all *together*? This is what makes conversations (and Bangkok traffic) difficult. This is what makes social comprehension messy.

As I write this book, with every changing global event that has occurred since its inception, my confidence to make even the most humble suggestions fluctuates. I'd be remiss to say that I have even a fraction of the answers; I have only the experiences that have shaped me. When tragedy strikes in any form, I am working to shift from frenziedly reacting to pausing and trying to be a better observer of the world. So I have begun paying closer and closer attention to the way humanity spins in response to tragedy. I've unpacked moments with family and friends in America and abroad. I have watched kids process news that comes their way in cities like New York, Chicago, Bangkok, and Singapore. I've listened to colleagues with expansive local and global educational backgrounds dissect news with their respective cultural and philosophical lenses, views shaped by their identity and experiences. All the while, I have been on the hunt for the constants. What is the same in the way the brilliant humans around me respond to what the world hands them? And how do I capture constants in a world where the only constant is change?

What Can We Do?

Here is my best collection of ways we can all be more compassionate observers of the world. Making these a part of who we are makes us at least a fraction more prepared when we face crisis together.

Understand That Everyone's Identity Is at Stake

Take any recent crisis that we have experienced as a society. List the perpetrator(s), bystander(s), victim(s), upstander(s). Consider the known and factual identities of all the people involved: How much do you know about them and their story beyond the

Figure 6.1 In the early months of 2017, during the US-imposed electronics ban on all flights direct from selected countries in the Middle East to the United States, I found myself on long plane trips without a laptop. Per my editor Tobey's advice, I planned much of this book in my journal, with colored pens, inspired by the sketch noting of Tanny McGregor. It did two things for me: one, made me a better observer of the world around me, and two, got me more proximate to my fellow passengers and their stories.

headlines? Now, consider the identities of the kids in your class, in the adult community of your school. Hold a mirror up to yourself as well. Are there identity connections or parallels to be drawn? I don't mean character here, I mean the foundational elements of identity. For me that means I am looking for anyone I can connect to as a female of color, daughter, sister, aunt, athlete, first-generation American, or offspring of immigrants.

Sometimes I may identify with the victims; other times I may identify with the perpetrators and the bystanders. That makes for a potentially difficult conversation with others, but I am cognizant of the fact that this is my reality. People who are mindful of the identities within their community pause as they plan how to divulge truths or explore news, knowing that everyone's identity is at stake. They aren't afraid. They don't avoid discussions of identity. Transformative progress is their goal and everyone is a solution.

Get Proximate to the Human Story

Bryan Stevenson, human rights activist, founder of the Equal Justice Initiative, and author of *Just Mercy*, tells people who want to help save the world to get proximate to problems. "If you are not proximate, you cannot change the world" (Stevenson 2015a).

We need to work on getting close to the stories of people who don't look like us, who are marginalized, who are living a reality we can't fathom.

We can absolutely use reading as a means to get a little closer and, as many say, to build empathy. Let's also be particular about the voices and authors who are telling those stories: Are these authors describing their own experience? If I choose to get proximate to the stories of refugees, I am going to work very hard to find first-person accounts, told by *that* refugee or someone who shared their experience with them rather than by an outsider.

In the event of any tragedy, shouldn't we be far less fascinated with the perpetrator's story (often glorified by the media) than with the stories of the victim(s) (rarely shared beyond a photo). Shouldn't the victims be the ones we are honoring with airtime? So we can look them and their loved ones in the face and say *never again*? Lives gone too soon against their will. Many of them children in whom we can see our own children if we see them first as people, like us, and only secondarily as victims, statistics—numbers of an unlucky group. When we ignore their realities, they are reduced to a quantitative measurement, a fatality number in a rising global toll. They are not remembered as the seven-year-old who loved drawing, playing with her siblings, and riding her bike.

The more people I watch who choose to get proximate—the couple who brought books to an apartment community that didn't otherwise have easy access to the public library; the teachers who visit refugee families in detention centers each week to play with their kids and create instructional lessons for them; the young man who brought his passion for photography to a forgotten neighborhood of Chicago, not to exploit them as subjects but to capture their choice of family photos and events, gratis—the more I know that this is the road to empathy. We can't distance ourselves. We have to get closer. And we especially have to get closer to the people who don't look like us.

Be an Authentic Listener

The very best listeners I have observed in life have a way of naturally disarming others in a difficult conversation without saying a word. As Harvard's Project Negotiation explains, "The heart of good listening is authenticity" (quoted in Patton et al. 2010, 167). Skilled listeners have a stance that shows the speaker that they care. You cannot fake this stance. You have to genuinely care and commit. This is why I implore teachers to ask kids what's in *their* news, not to impose only our own news on them. If we face tragedy together, we cannot force an agenda on them and then be upset when they "aren't listening." When we allow kids to be curious about topics they care and wonder about, and when we are honest with them, they give their whole selves to the listening. And if we enter into a brave conversation with someone, we must commit to the path it may take and be authentic in our listening so we send the message that the other person's ideas, thoughts, and feelings are legitimized. My bet is your commitment will be reciprocated.

Get Out of Your Echo Chamber

In an article in *Wired* magazine entitled, "Your Filter Bubble is Destroying Democracy," writer Mostafa M. El-Bermawy (2016) argues, "The global village that was once the internet has been replaced by digital islands of isolation that are drifting further apart each day." It is true. Ever wondered how Google, Amazon, Facebook, and virtually any ad you encounter on the Internet is exactly what you were thinking about or interested in? Our Internet life, thanks to analytics, is becoming increasingly personalized—and polarized.

That same article cites the Pew Center's research on how many millennials use Facebook as their primary news source about politics and government: 61 percent. Yes, Facebook, the same platform where people share adorable pet and holiday photos, is millennials' main resource for information on national and global issues. Of course it is convenient when everything comes in a neatly organized, attractive, blue-logoed package where all of your friends and acquaintances also hang out. People align themselves with and are drawn to people who look and think like themselves. However, to understand local and global issues and shocking tragedies that rip through communities, we have to get outside of our echo chambers.

We can start to get out of our bubbles by taking stock: Who are you following on social media? What books and blogs are you reading? Who are the voices of your podcasts, both those speaking and those discussed? Do you know stories or have personal experiences that counter the fear-spreading narratives surrounding those portrayed as perpetrators or as victims, and those who have been edged to the margins of society? Listening to a wide array of voices reminds us that there are people who can think and feel like us while having drastically different points of view. And you can't click on the "block" button when standing face to face with someone.

Measure the Inclusiveness of Your Community

When crisis strikes, when news calls for brave conversations, who are the people we call resources? Who are the people in our circles of trust?

Now consider: Who in that circle looks different from you? Do you have the perspectives of anyone who is directly involved or anyone whose identity overlaps with the identities of those involved in the incident? For example: There is a shooting of a(nother) black teenager by white police officers. This topic comes up in your social media feeds, your communities, your classrooms. Whose voices do you hear? Do these voices offer you a full perspective on the depth and multiple layers of the situation?

If we choose to be immersed in a narrow chamber of perspective, we will have a difficult time getting beyond comments like, "Oh, that is so sad" or "I just can't believe it." These words may convey concern or dismay, but they don't help anyone to better understand a situation or to take action to improve it. For every time that we may have the privilege of distance to say something is "sad," there is someone or a community of people living the experience. Sometimes over and over again.

Commit to a Learning Stance

Committing to a learning stance is not just going into a conversation ready to listen; it is going into a conversation ready to *learn*. Essentially, this means you are confident that you don't know everything, that you will uncover your own misconceptions, and that you will walk away from the conversation having more knowledge (facts, perspective, emotions, compassion, thinking) than you started with. It means you are evolved enough to say, "I know my truths but I am going to listen and accept what this other person is saying as also a truth. I am going to listen—not to respond, but to learn something I didn't know before."

When you begin by considering where there are gaps in your understanding, you will find that you have more developed questions than binary ones. You are constructing knowledge that can be open-ended and nonjudgmental. Try it with a history that is not your own or that doesn't center on you. Then you say to yourself, "OK, I have this newly constructed knowledge formed not only by my own identity and experiences, but also by new perspectives, new voices, personal misconceptions, differing opinions, and more questions. What do I do with what I now know?"

A learning stance is the most difficult when we find it the most challenging to be an effective listener. Keep in mind that this is not the time to boast your strengths. This is the time for you to work through your vulnerabilities and discomfort and take on some responsibility. This is not an easy stance, but it leads us to much-needed growth: history continues to wait for change as it repeats itself time and time again. It's time to hold ourselves accountable.

Shine a Spotlight on the Upstanders

As Mr. Rogers' mom told him as a boy when he was frightened by the news, "Always look for the helpers." See "Tragic Events" (https://www.fredrogers.org/parents/special-challenges/tragic-events.php).

There is so much good in this world.

It is worth saying again: there is so much good in this world.

Watch any local news channel and count the minutes that are spent on negative and tragic news. Then there is a segment at the end that is supposed to be uplifting after twenty-eight minutes of doom and fear-mongering. What if we spent time looking for, amplifying, and creating space for the upstanders? After the bombings in cities like Paris and Manchester, stories or hashtags pop up that show how ordinary people are helping others: letting them borrow a cell phone, giving them a place of refuge or a free ride. We don't see this in the mainstream media. It is up to us to help our kids feel safe by shining a spotlight on all those people who do good, who lift us up from the rubble.

Be Proactive with Your Privilege

We are a responsive culture. Laws are often created in response to something. Too many reported injuries and fatalities yield seatbelt and helmet laws. Educational laws (like IDEA) usually surface from a lawsuit or court case. People are rightfully outraged in response to another shooting at a school or religious institution, yet we continue to allow hate speech and irresponsible gun laws to hide behind our Bill of Rights. We protest *after* another innocent black person is killed by police. But when the dust settles, and a couple weeks pass by, we are back to our regularly scheduled program. Until the next atrocity comes along.

Consider the times that you have been proactive about even the most ordinary things. You did your shopping early. You got holiday cards out ahead of the game. You bought school supplies at the right time rather than in the stampede a week before school. How did being proactive change the course or outcomes for you? Maybe the holidays were less stressful. Maybe you were calmer and more organized on the first day of school. Maybe things went the way you wanted them to go.

While we can't plan ahead for reacting to a crisis, we can proactively practice what we preach and what we tweet. We can stay informed, raise awareness, and advocate. We can be activists beyond 140 characters and status updates. What can be done between the phases of outrage? What small acts can we shift day to day? What can we read that offers a different perspective? Whom can we talk to or forge a friendship with outside of our current circles of trust? Whom can we call to make change? What or whom can we stand up to, in the meantime? Author Brendan Kiely writes in his book with Jason Reynolds, *All American Boys*, "There are no bystanders. We all have a role" (2015).

What are you doing in your school and classroom that will help you prepare for, prevent, or respond to the next tragedy that comes our way? How are you talking to your kids about bigotry, about race and racism? What news do you hear kids bringing into the room? What writing and reading can you do on your own or with your students and colleagues that will help make *next time* further along in the conversation? We must be proactive with our privilege.

Progress with Compassion

Educators are experts. We are researchers, intellectuals, and civic actors. We are on the front lines of ensuring the health and safety of our kids each and every day. Yet, we are often told to detach ourselves from the issues that directly impact their lives. While this expectation might help us to keep compliant classrooms and stay on schedule, it stymies our compassion, throws off our ethical compass, and does our kids a grave disservice. We need to engage with the issues that our future generations care about.

It's true that we do not have all the answers for them. But we can support kids in learning more about the bigger themes, lessons, and questions they are asking to explore.

We can listen genuinely and allow our kids to have honest discussions with one another. We can embolden them to ask their questions when something doesn't feel right or to look at issues in the world around them with a skeptical lens. We can affirm their identities and their communities. We can model for our students the power of compassion, of speaking up in the face of injustice, and of making the choice to be brave—even when it is hard. We can celebrate our diversity and strive for just inclusivity. We need all voices on deck. As professor, scholar, and author Sonia Nieto (2013) reminds us, *teaching is an ethical endeavor*. We cannot afford to remove *ethics* from *education*. We cannot continue to experience the implications of its absence.

It's Up to Us

My parents raised me to do small things with a big heart.

I'll bet someone inspired you to kindness and action, too.

I am a hopeless optimist. I'll bet you are, too.

I am convinced that every class of kids I work with is filled with change agents who will make this world the one we teach toward. I believe that my students will carry the work of doing right by this world into their own lives.

I'll bet you believe this about your kids, too.

There is no magic formula for making the world a better place. It happens in the moments we break our silent complicity, embrace discomfort, and have candid conversations about what stands in the way. As educators, you and I are tasked with giving kids opportunities to show compassion, to be upstanders, and to realize the impact they have in society. It's an awe-inspiring responsibility, but it's something that you and I—people who believe in kids—are uniquely qualified to undertake.

Suggested Resource Stacks

Educators frequently ask me for lists of media resources to use when teaching social comprehension. The resources below are some of the tools I turn to most often in this work.

Picture Books
Ada Twist, Scientist; Rosie Revere, Engineer; and *Iggy Peck, Architect* by Andrea Beaty
Amelia and Eleanor Go for a Ride by Pam Munoz Ryan
Chrysanthemum by Kevin Henkes
Each Kindness by Jacqueline Woodson
Harvesting Hope: The Story of Cesar Chavez by Kathleen Krull
The Invisible Boy by Tracy Ludwig
Jacob's New Dress by Sarah and Ian Hoffman
Langston's Train Ride by Robert Burleigh
The Librarian of Basra by Jeanette Winter
Malala, a Brave Girl from Pakistan and *Iqbal, a Brave Boy from Pakistan: Two Stories of Bravery* by Jeanette Winter
The Man Who Walked Between the Towers by Mordicai Gerstein
Manfish: A Story of Jacques Cousteau by Jennifer Berne
Mirror by Jeannie Baker
My Name Is Bilal by Asma Mobin-Uddin
My Name Is Elizabeth! by Annika Dunklee
My Name Is Yoon by Helen Recorvits
The Name Jar by Yangsook Choi
Sunday Chutney by Aaron Blabey
Stella Brings the Family by Miriam B. Schiffer
Thunder Boy Jr. by Sherman Alexie
The Youngest Marcher by Cynthia Levinson

Poetry
"Phenomenal Woman" by Maya Angelou
Bravo! Poems About Amazing Hispanics by Margarita Engle
Out of Wonder: Poems Celebrating Poets by Kwame Alexander with Chris Colderley and Marjory Wentworth

Selections from the verse novels *Out of the Dust* by Karen Hesse or *Bronx Masquerade* by Nikki Grimes

The opening page of *Caminar*, a novel in verse, by Skila Brown (the page is titled "Where I'm From")

Short Stories
"Thank You, Ma'am" by Langston Hughes
"The Lottery" by Shirley Jackson
"The Scholarship Jacket" by Marta Salinas
"Raymond's Run" by Toni Cade Bambara
"Seventh Grade" by Gary Soto
"The Other Side" by Jacqueline Woodson

Short Story Anthologies
America Street: A Multicultural Anthology of Stories edited by Anne Mazer
First Crossings: Stories About Teen Immigrants edited by Donald R. Gallo
Flying Lessons edited by Ellen Oh
The Paper Menagerie and Other Stories by Ken Liu
When I Was Your Age: Original Stories About Growing Up, Volumes I and II, edited by Amy Ehrlich

Novels
Any Small Goodness: A Novel of the Barrio by Tony Johnston
Refugee by Alan Gratz
Seedfolks by Paul Fleischman

Nonfiction
"Orientation Day" by Jennifer Wang
The Sunflower by Simon Wiesenthal

Videos
"Not in Our Town: Billings Montana," niot.org
"The Bystander" by Osnat Epstein

References and Inspiration

Beers, G. Kylene, and Robert E. Probst. 2017. *Disrupting Thinking: Why How We Read Matters*. New York: Scholastic.

"Best News Sources for Kids." 1970. Common Sense Media. January 1. www .commonsensemedia.org/lists/best-news-sources-for-kids.

Cherry-Paul, Sonja, Cornelius Minor, and Sara K. Ahmed. 2017. "Dismantling Racism in Education." *Heinemann Blog* (audio blog), June 23. www.heinemann.com/blog /the-heinemann-podcast-dismantling-racism-in-education.

Cisneros, Sandra. *The House on Mango Street*. New York: Vintage Books, 1991, c1989.

"Cornelius Minor on Being an Advocate for your Students." 2017. Interview. *Heinemann Podcasts* (audio blog), April 28. www.heinemann.com/blog/the- heinemann-podcast-cornelius-minor-on-being-an-advocate-for-your-students.

Daniels, Harvey. 2017. *The Curious Classroom: 10 Structures for Teaching with Student-Directed Inquiry*. Portsmouth, NH: Heinemann.

Daniels, Harvey, and Sara K. Ahmed. 2015. *Upstanders: How to Engage Middle School Hearts and Minds with Inquiry*. Portsmouth, NH: Heinemann.

Daniels, Harvey, and Elaine Daniels. 2013. *The Best-Kept Teaching Secret: How Written Conversations Engage Kids, Activate Learning, Grow Fluent Writers*. Thousand Oaks, CA: Corwin.

Daniels, Harvey, and Nancy Steineke. 2004. *Mini-Lessons for Literature Circles*. Portsmouth, NH: Heinemann.

Darling-Hammond, Linda. 2001. *The Right to Learn: A Blueprint for Creating Schools That Work*. San Francisco: Jossey-Bass.

El-Bermawy, Mostafa. 2016. "Your Filter Bubble Is Destroying Democracy." *Wired*. November 18. www.wired.com/2016/11/filter-bubble-destroying-democracy.

Facing History and Ourselves. www.facinghistory.org.

———. Lesson 2: "Universe of Obligation." www.facinghistory.org/resource-library /universal-declaration-human-rights/universe-obligation.

Finson, Kevin D. 2002. "Drawing a Scientist: What We Do and Do Not Know After Fifty Years of Drawings." *School Science and Mathematics*. November. http://onlinelibrary .wiley.com/doi/10.1111/j.1949-8594.2002.tb18217.x/abstract.

Freire, Paulo. 2000. *Pedagogy of the Oppressed*. Translated by Myra Bergman Ramos. London: Bloomsbury Academic.

Fried, Robert L. 2001. *The Passionate Teacher: A Practical Guide*. Boston: Beacon Press.

Glover, Matt, and Mary Alice Berry. 2012. *Projecting Possibilities for Writers: The How, What and Why of Designing Units of Study, K–5*. Portsmouth, NH: Heinemann.

138

Glover, Matt, and Ellin Oliver Keene. 2015. *The Teacher You Want to Be: Essays About Children, Learning and Teaching.* Portsmouth, NH: Heinemann.

Graves, Donald H. 2006. *A Sea of Faces: The Importance of Knowing Your Students.* Portsmouth, NH: Heinemann.

Hanson, Rick. 2010. "How Did Humans Become Empathic?" *Your Wise Brain* (blog). *Psychology Today.* March 3. www.psychologytoday.com/blog/your-wise-brain/201003/how-did-humans-become-empathic.

Harvey, Stephanie, and Harvey Daniels. 2015. *Comprehension & Collaboration: Inquiry Circles for Curiosity, Engagement, and Understanding.* Portsmouth, NH: Heinemann.

Harvey, Stephanie, and Anne Goudvis. 2016. *The Intermediate Comprehension Toolkit.* 2nd edition. Portsmouth, NH: Heinemann.

Johnston, Peter H. 2012. *Opening Minds: Using Language to Change Lives.* Portland, ME: Stenhouse.

Jones, Richard, and Arthur Bangert. 2006. "The CSI Effect: Changing the Face of Science." *Science Scope*, November, 38–42. http://static.nsta.org/files/ss0611_38.pdf.

Katz, A. J. 2016. "Why 'Black Man, White America' Became 'United Shades of America.'" TVNewser. June 3. www.adweek.com/tvnewser/why-black-man-white-america-became-united-shades-of-america/295106.

Kiely, Brendan, and Jason Reynolds. 2015. *All American Boys.* New York: Simon & Schuster.

Kozol, Jonathan. 2004. *Savage Inequalities: Children in America's Schools.* New York: HarperPerennial.

Lyon, George Ella. "Where I'm From." www.georgeellalyon.com/where.html.

Making Caring Common Project. 2014. *The Children We Mean to Raise: The Real Messages Adults Are Sending About Values.* Harvard Graduate School of Education. https://mcc.gse.harvard.edu/files/gse-mcc/files/mcc-executive-summary.pdf.

McGregor, Tanny. 2007. *Comprehension Connections: Bridges to Strategic Reading.* Portsmouth, NH: Heinemann.

Miller, Donalyn. 2015. "The House That Reading Built." *Nerdy Book Club* (blog), November 15. https://nerdybookclub.wordpress.com/2015/11/15/the-house-that-reading-built-by-donalyn-miller.

Mraz, Kristine, and Christine Hertz. 2015. *A Mindset for Learning: Teaching the Traits of Joyful, Independent Growth.* Portsmouth, NH: Heinemann.

Muhtaris, Katie, and Kristin Ziemke. 2015. *Amplify: Digital Teaching and Learning in the K–6 Classroom.* Portsmouth, NH: Heinemann.

Newkirk, Thomas. 2014. *Minds Made for Stories: How We Really Read and Write Informational and Persuasive Texts.* Portsmouth, NH: Heinemann.

Nieto, Sonia. 2009. *Language, Culture, and Teaching: Critical Perspectives.* 2nd edition. New York: Routledge.

———. 2013. *Finding Joy in Teaching Students of Diverse Backgrounds: Culturally Responsive and Socially Just Practices in U.S. Classrooms*. Portsmouth, NH: Heinemann.

Patton, Bruce, Douglas Stone, and Sheila Heen. 2010. *Difficult Conversations: How to Discuss What Matters Most*, 10th anniversary edition. London: Penguin, 2010.

Probst, Robert E. 2004. *Response and Analysis: Teaching Literature in Secondary School*. Portsmouth, NH: Heinemann.

Reshamwala, Saleem. "Who, Me? Biased? Peanut Butter, Jelly and Racism." *New York Times* POV video. www.nytimes.com/video/us/100000004818663/peanut-butter-jelly-and -racism.html?playlistId=100000004821064.

Ripp, Pernille. 2018. *Passionate Readers: The Art of Reaching and Engaging Every Child*. New York: Routledge.

Roberts, Terrence J. 2013. *Lessons from Little Rock*. Little Rock, AR: Butler Center Books.

Sanfey, Alan G., and Luke J. Chang. 2008. "Of Two Minds When Making a Decision." *Scientific American*. June 3. www.scientificamerican.com/article/of-two-minds-when -making.

Schein, Edgar H. 2014. *Humble Inquiry: The Gentle Art of Asking Instead of Telling*. San Francisco: Berrett-Koehler.

Singleton, Glenn E., and James P. Comer. 2013. *More Courageous Conversations About Race*. Thousand Oaks, CA: Corwin Press.

Stanton, Gregory H. 2018. Personal correspondence.

Stevenson, Bryan. 2012. "We Need to Talk About Injustice." TED Talk, TED2012. www .ted.com/talks/bryan_stevenson_we_need_to_talk_about_an_injustice.

———. 2015a. Keynote address at benefit for Facing History and Ourselves, November 5, New York.

———. 2015b. *Just Mercy: A Story of Justice and Redemption*. Melbourne, Victoria: Scribe.

Strom, Margot Stern. 1994. *Facing History and Ourselves: Holocaust and Human Behavior Resource Book*. Brookline, MA: Facing History and Ourselves National Foundation.

Sue, Derald Wing. 2010. "Microaggressions: More Than Just Race." *Psychology Today*. November 17.

"Tragic Events." Parent Resources—Tragic Events. Accessed February 9, 2018. https://www.fredrogers.org/parents/special-challenges/tragic-events.php.

Vilson, Jose. 2015. "The Teacher You Want to Be: Jose Vilson on Difficult Conversations." *Heinemann Blog*, December 9. www.heinemann.com/blog/vilson-tuwant2b-12-9.

Walsh, Colleen. 2014. "Layers of Choice." *Harvard Gazette*. February 5. https://news .harvard.edu/gazette/story/2014/02/layers-of-choice/#pq=v10mwP.

Winter, Jeanette. 2005. *The Librarian of Basra: A True Story from Iraq*. Orlando, FL: Harcourt.